MW01595589

A HAVEN BEFORE HEAVEN

The Untold Story of Relentless Determination

Stefanie Held

Dedicated to my hero, my husband "Maury" Maurice Louis Held.

In memory of my parents Beverly and Albert Sidd and my courageous grandson, Nathanial Louis Arnold

Some names have been changed to protect the confidentiality of people with AIDS. All details are written to the best of my recollection.

The painting on the cover is Stefanie Held's interpretation of the "Women with AIDS Support Group" and was designed by Chris Arnold: chris@eyeconmurals.com

Thank you to my literary agent, Jean Kerr, Chris Arnold, Paul Riddle, Carrie Temple, and photographer Lisa Means who took the black and white photos featured in the book: lisameans.com (214) 826-4079.

Table of Contents

"I believe to meet the challenge of the next century; human beings will have to develop a greater sense of universal responsibility. Each of us must learn to work not just for his or her own self, family or nation, but for the benefit of all mankind."

-The Dalai Lama

A DEATH-DEFYING ACT

In the 1980s, Ronald Reagan was President. The rise of conservatism in social, economic and political life was gaining in popularity. Computers, mobile phones, and DNA profiling were all in their infancy. It was a time of innovative technology which would alter our daily existence forever. Few knew, during these times of extraordinary metamorphoses, a disease called Acquired Immune Deficiency Syndrome (AIDS) was lurking in the shadows and spreading across America.

Early on, most accounts of the disease focused on the devastating plight of gay men with the disease. The deadly new epidemic was being spread from one man to another, deeply puzzling the medical community. The crisis seemed to emerge out of nowhere, seemingly uncontrollable and was unlike anything the United States had ever experienced. With an initial airborne theory, the epidemic caused a perplexing phenomenon, instilling fear nationwide.

Men were dying in astounding numbers, and the medical community could not figure out the origin of the disease or how it was being spread. Initially, because AIDS was thought to be almost exclusively a gay man's disease, it was not given sufficient attention from the medical community, researchers, or the government until it was of epidemic proportions.

AIDS was considered to be mysteriously contagious, and life-threatening. Numerous theories were contemplated while men were becoming very ill and inevitably dying. As the disease spread across our country in unprecedented numbers, doctors began realizing the magnitude of the disease. The search for answers became imperative.

In the quest for answers, doctors began recognizing a specific set of visible symptoms might indicate the newly identified disease was the probable cause. A skin cancer which caused oozing sores and wasting syndrome which caused the body to become extremely thin and frail were often signs a person was infected. These frightful and apparent manifestations of the disease, evoked fear in others, resulting in the isolation of these men at a time when compassion was most needed.

Identifying the mode of transmission was essential in developing a defense against the spread of the disease. After some time, the conclusion was the exchange of bodily fluids was the vehicle which was transferring the virus from one person to another. Although the medical community was finally confident they understood how the disease was being transmitted, society at large had little confidence in the findings and continued to fear any contact with those who could potentially be infected. Initially, there was rampant fear which seemed justified because so many questions remained unanswered. The panic resulted in a reluctance to care for the sick and dying.

Out of necessity, gay activists became proactive themselves and demanded action from the medical community and the government. Without much support from society, they began organizing and forming support systems to meet the needs of the infected men. They rallied volunteers to care for the sick and established organizations to raise funds for research. They intensely searched for and obtained experimental drugs hoping to find some relief for the infected.

As the momentum of the disease increased, my husband Maury and I became aware of this life-crushing disease in the gay community. We were compelled to do whatever was needed to help the people who were being struck by this horrific illness. The fact that it was primarily gay men made little difference to us. People were dying, and they needed help.

The media was continually highlighting the numbers of the newly diagnosed and the deaths of prominent people with the disease. Many were the creative people of our times. Often, they were the authors, actors, artists, poets, and designers. As artists, Maury and I had many friends in the affected community, and we observed the devastation of the disease first hand. In addition to raising money for services and research, we began helping to care for the sick and dying in ways most people avoided because of the fear of the unknowns. We were in a minority of people who were not gay who joined the front lines of the battle. We brought assistance to the bedridden and joined organizations which were forming to help the infected. We volunteered at fundraisers and participated in efforts to improve the quality of life for those who were suffering. We held the hands of people as their life drifted away from them. We were committed to helping out wherever we could to make a difference during this tragic epidemic.

In the mid-1980s, Maury and I heard whisperings about a previously unknown population of people who were also being devastated by this mysterious disease: families and children. Few were aware, amid the chaos of the gay men's outbreak, AIDS was also infecting mothers, fathers, and children. This minority population of the infected was suffering in silence and hiding in their homes in fear of anyone finding out they were carrying the dreaded disease. These families were relegated to live in the shadows of the gay men's crisis. Much like the male population, they were gravely ill, but also, many of these families had spouses and children who were also infected. Unlike the gay community, these families were living isolated without a community of support to help them. As they were suffering in silence, they were also living in fear of the persecution which was raining down on everyone with HIV/AIDS.

Families affected by AIDS began increasing in number and gathering attention. It was becoming more widely known that women and children were also vulnerable to the wrath of this deadly disease. Still, the number of men with AIDS far exceeded the number of families and children affected by the disease and consequently this minority populations needs were ignored in any services which were being developed to provide assistance.

Entire families were living through a life-crushing disease which would inevitably end all their lives, and most were all alone in their struggle. Their needs were different than those of single men therefore, already established support services, did not accommodate families and children. There were many circumstances which necessitated intervention and support for the affected children and families to cope with the devastating effects of the disease. Parents needed assistance caring for their children when they were too debilitated to care for them. They needed a place their children could stay, night or day, sometimes for a few hours or a few days, to alleviate the toll on an ill parent trying to care for an ill child, and nothing was available to assist them. Often the parents did not know how to meet the daily medical needs of their sick and dying children and needed a place where their child could get proper out of hospital care. Periodically, ill parents needed someone to care for their infected and well children when the parent was in the hospital. Parents often needed assistance in finding social services for the basic needs of daily survival. In the early stages of the disease, when parents were well enough to work, they required childcare for their infected children who were banned from traditional childcare. The families continuously needed support to help them cope with the complex demands of a terminal family. Families desperately needed a support system free from persecution and judgment. A place where they were accepted and not isolated. A place where their plight was understood.

In addition to families, infants were being born to infected mothers who were unable or unwilling to care for their newborns. Newborns suspected of having the disease were being abandoned at birth and left to live out their lives in hospitals. Thousands of children were becoming orphans when their parents died from the illness, and because of the fear which existed, and the complicated nature of the disease, no foster parents were willing to accept these children.

The first family who Maury and I became acquainted with, who had multiple family members with the disease, opened our eyes to the complexities of families living with AIDS. We thought we had already experienced the epitome of the devastation which was caused when AIDS rained down on a person, but we soon learned about the horrific impact it had on an entire family.

When we met this family, we learned Lydia, Scott and their two sons Matthew and Bryan were fleeing their home in Colorado. They were moving to escape the persecution they had been experiencing in the town where they had been living. Without hesitation, Maury and I befriended the family when they arrived in our area. We became fast friends and learned the heartbreaking story of a family struggling with a disease which ravaged their bodies and would ultimately kill each one of them. An illness which debilitated their family in every way. An illness which ostracized them from society. A disease which had no treatment or cure. Life was literally being sucked out of these people's lives, and we became determined to find some way to ease their pain while they endured the horrific devastation of this cruel disease.

Lydia and I became close friends, and as our friendship evolved, we began to hear about other families who were living in isolation and struggling to maintain their lives. We reached out to them and tried to provide help in whatever way we could. As time went on more families came out of the darkness and sought out our help. The number of children and families kept increasing, and so did their needs. It pretty quickly became apparent that we could not provide the amount of help which was needed by ourselves.

It became my mission to figure out a plan which assisted with the complex needs of children and families and provide them with some quality of life while they were enduring this nightmare. I had confidence that with enough focus on the problems that they were dealing with, I could come up with a support system which would encompass the many needs of these families.

Together, Lydia and I began to figure out a support system which would help infected families and orphaned children. These families were dealing with so many varied problems it was complicated to figure out a solution which would encompass all the different aspects of a support system which would meet their needs, but I was passionately determined.

Lydia was a nurse and had her personal experience with the disease. I was the idea person, a creative thinker, with a can-do attitude. Together we began constructing a unique care system which would meet the ever-changing needs of children and families with AIDS.

Without any prior experience in starting a non-profit organization, we figured out what was needed and forged forward. In the beginning, we had no funding source or any idea how we would find the immense amount of money it would take to finance our grandiose plan. Organizations around the country were still in the very early planning stages of trying to contend with the needs of this population, so there were no models to follow. Every step to accomplish the vision was complicated. It took immense persistence, and the obsessive hard work was endless.

Ultimately, the solution became a refuge which would be a constant source of assistance whenever a child or parent affected by AIDS was in need. The complexities of the kind of help they needed varied throughout the disease and a flexible plan of care were necessary to accommodate all the possible variables. We concluded we needed to provide a place, with a homelike atmosphere, which would function as a safety net for children while offering support services to the families.

On November 20, 1988, we opened the doors to the first home which provided a comprehensive continuum of care for children and families affected by HIV/AIDS. The home provided medically managed day care, respite care and permanent residential care for children while incorporating support services for the entire family. We successfully defied the doubters who thought what we were trying to do was seemingly impossible.

The home was named Bryan's House in honor of Lydia's son Bryan, who was the first child known to die from perinatally acquired AIDS in the Dallas/Fort Worth area. Bryan's House became recognized nationally and internationally as the first comprehensive model program providing care to medically fragile children and their families with HIV/AIDS.

Opening the doors to Bryan's House was only the beginning of the long road of overcoming obstacles, trudging through bureaucracies and figuratively climbing over mountains of resistance.

From deep down in my soul, compassion drove me to figure out a path to ease the deep and abiding suffering of strangers caught in the web of this deadly disease. What I didn't realize at the time, coming up with a plan to help, was only the beginning of this miraculous journey.

Stefanie Held with three children who benefitted from the services at Bryan's House.

1

DESTINY BLOOMING

Boston, Massachusetts, where I grew up, is a hub of inspiration. The city is flooded with colleges and universities. A place where people from all over the world gather to cultivate their aspirations. The atmosphere is filled with anticipation of exploration, paralleling Boston's deeply rooted beginnings. During the sixties, my most formative years, I was immersed in a population of students who had an intense thirst for knowledge. It was a time when young adults were inspired to create change by defying the existing norms. The environment was saturated with people whose ambition was to fulfill their desire to accomplish innovative idealistic ideas. Influenced by the intensity of an inspiring setting, during a decade which empowered change, I was infused with the confidence that I too could change the world.

Growing up in that inspiring environment and being the daughter of a prolific artist and wrestler, my childhood was not exactly conventional. Upon returning from the military, my dad decided to further his career by going to art school while my mother, a kindergarten teacher, supported the family. Unable to afford child care for me, each day I trotted off to art school with my dad. He would pack our lunches and off we'd go. At two years old I was exposed to an adult world of creative and diverse people. As I grew older, my destiny seemed to be that I would become an artist as well. During my teenage years, I planned to go to art school when I graduated high school. I fantasized about moving to Manhattan and living in Greenwich Village to pursue my painting career. The Village then was known as a stepping stone for struggling artists to become recognized. I had it all planned out in my mind of how I was going to live my life. Typically, I would set a path for myself, and I would set forth to accomplish it. I believed (and still do think) if people can imagine an idea and are willing to work hard enough, they can achieve their goals.

Becoming a serious artist was my life's plan, but as so often happens, life didn't work out exactly the way I planned.

My dream of moving to New York to pursue my art career was suddenly altered. In the fall of 1965, when New England was beginning her annual show of leaves with their magnificent colors, I met the love of my life.

At the start of each new school year, Boston was alive with excitement and anticipation as the youth of our country arrived to attend one of the many educational institutions which would teach them how to accomplish their dreams. For many, it was the milestone which would prepare them to lay the groundwork to become the movers and shakers of our time. The energy of dreams was darting everywhere, and each fall the atmosphere felt like a lightning storm. As the extraordinarily colorful leaves of a Boston autumn danced from the wind, they seemed to sense the electricity of hope in the air.

Every fall, venues were created by educational leaders to facilitate interaction between the novices and the experienced. College students were meeting strangers from every walk of life. Potential professional and social connections were blooming everywhere, creating relationships which would change lives. Society's brilliant people were collaborating to change our world. The air in the 1960s was filled with the hope that with action, injustice could be conquered. Consumed by optimism, all the old rules were being tested and pushed to their limits.

The fall of my senior year at Brookline High School was a time of excitement and anticipation for me. I was finally getting closer to participate in the dynamic environment which I grew up yearning to be a part of. The closer I got, the less patience I had to wait for what I perceived to be the beginning of my next chapter.

While the vivid leaves began to fall, revealing trees full of naked limbs, I decided to attend a mixer at Boston University with my best friend, Valerie. A "mixer" was the contemporary word for a social event, a meet and greet for college freshman. Being anxious to experience what was to come in our freshman year, Valerie and I made plans to go to the mixer despite the fact we were still in high school. We primped for hours, picking out appropriate clothing which we thought a college freshman might wear. We were confident our camouflage would disguise us from being recognized as high school students.

As we entered the crowded event, which was taking place at the student union, we were very relieved a student ID was not required for admission. Trying not to reveal our timid high school persona, we mingled and carried on conversations. Before long, I spotted a boy across the room who made my heart skip a beat. He had very dark hair, a tan which looked like it had been obtained with perfection, and a sparkle in his mesmerizing hazel eyes.

Nonchalantly, I made my way across the room to inconspicuously listen to the conversation he was having with his friends. I was intent on overhearing some information which I could use to start a conversation with him. I overheard this strikingly handsome person talking about a sculpture he had just completed. My heart started pounding, and I was sure I was in love.

His name was Maury, short for Maurice. He was stunning to look at and an artist also! Could I have just found the love of my life?

During my eavesdropping, I overheard the group talking about all the "high school Harriet's" at the event. After Val and I infiltrated their conversation, someone in the group asked what school I was attending. Without hesitation, a lie freely rolled off my tongue, and I answered Lesley University College of Art and Design. It was one of the schools I was hoping to get into in the following fall. The boys invited us back to the fraternity house for an after party. We crammed into the crowded car for the short ride to the party. Val and I had to sit on somebody's lap for us all to fit in the car. I had no doubt whose lap I was going to end up on. The fraternity house was located on one of Boston's picturesque tree-lined streets overlooking the famous Charles River. This quintessential majestic townhouse was typical of the Beacon Hill area where most of the Boston University fraternity houses were. When we arrived, the letters on the oversized purple door identified it as the Tau Epsilon Phi fraternity. The setting fit perfectly into the fantasy of a storybook romance. The whole evening was filled with endless excitement, exceeding any expectations I had anticipated for that night. The evening transformed the trajectory of my life. By the time the evening was over, I was sure I was in love. When I got home, I promptly woke my mother to tell her I had met the person I was going to marry!

On January 22, 1967, of the following year, we were married. I was 19 and Maury was 20 years old. My generation was raised to believe women should be conciliatory to her husband, and in many cases, it meant losing her identity in the process. For us, our "love at first sight" romance became a genuine partnership. We were undeniable equals in our relationship. We were each other's biggest supporters and always had each other's back. We were two parts of a whole. When people would ask Maury what he attributed the success of our marriage too, he would always give the same answer "treat each other with kindness." We lived by that astute statement.

Maury was a sophomore at Boston University by then, and I was in art school. Maury planned to go to law school after he finished undergraduate school. We had a long road of intentions and plans to accomplish the goals toward our future. As the unpredictability of life would have it, I got pregnant three months after we were married.

Our first child, Kimberly An (no, not a typo, just my propensity to be different), was born 7 days after our first anniversary. I became pregnant with our second child, Joshua Adam, in Maury's last year of Law school.

During my pregnancy with Kim, I spent my time volunteering at a state institution for abandoned children with severe disabilities. Most of the children who were confined there were severely deformed as a result of their mothers taking a drug called Thalidomide while they were pregnant. A medication which was prescribed as a sedative, purporting to alleviate morning sickness in pregnant women. Amongst other deformities, Thalidomide caused the children to be born without any or partially deformed limbs. These children were castoffs as a result of the medical community's mistake. Many were warehoused in institutions hidden from the public's site. When I heard about these children, I was compelled to give them love and attention. It was an especially disturbing experience for me because it heightened my concerns about my own baby growing inside of me, but I couldn't turn away from these orphaned children. These institutionalized children so desperately needed someone who would look past their disfiguring abnormalities and give them the individual attention which all kids deserve. The images of those poor forgotten children will live in my heart forever.

Maury, the children, and I moved to New Jersey when Maury graduated from Boston University Law School. He went to work on Wall Street at the Securities and Exchange Commission. I stayed home and took care of our two young children during the day and took classes at Rutgers University at night. After two years of Maury's commuting to New York and spending many hours in underground transportation, never seeing the light of day, or more importantly the children and me, we decided to make a change, and we moved to the land of sunshine. We arrived in Dallas in 1973.

Shortly after we settled in Dallas, I caught a cold which evolved into a respiratory infection which lingered for months getting progressively worse as time went on. My lungs were constricted, and every breath was labored. I saw numerous doctors and was given enormous amounts of steroids to no avail. As the months went on, I became more incapacitated and was admitted to the Pulmonary Care Unit of the hospital. I spent the next full year in the hospital struggling to breathe. Doctors were mystified because the conventional treatments had no effect. I was on the brink of death, and all they knew to do was to keep increasing the already unusually high doses of steroids which they had been giving me.

The immense amounts of steroids began to break down my body. They caused my bones to become brittle, and I fractured my back just bending over. My body filled with fluid as the result of the steroids, making getting around challenging. Being immobile from the combination of the excess fluid and the fractures led to pneumonia, compromising my ability to breathe even more. My pituitary gland shut down from the overuse of the steroids. I was in a downward spiral struggling to hang on to life. I believed, and the doctors thought, I was dying, and it seemed there was no way to change the inevitable.

As I lay in my bed in the ICU listening to doctors contemplating putting me on life support, it occurred to me that maybe the steroids were to blame for the downward spiral. It seemed the more they gave me, the sicker I became. The doctors strongly disagreed. I grew adamant about stopping the steroids. Being adamant about anything at the time was a challenge in my weakened condition. The doctors informed me that abruptly stopping the steroids would be life-threatening because my pituitary gland was no longer functioning as a result of the steroids, and if I stopped taking them, I would certainly die. As I lay there, each breath became harder and harder. Maury stood there begging me to take one more breath after another hoping to hold off the doctors from putting me on life support. I refused any more steroids and decided whatever happened was better than how I was living. Dying was a more welcome alternative than living the way I was.

One of the doctors who was taking care of me in the ICU was from Canada. He told me about an experimental drug being used there which might help my pituitary gland to start functioning again, but it was not approved for use in the United States. This dedicated young doctor said if I agreed to continue the steroids temporarily, he would get on a plane that same day to get the drug and be back the next day to administer it. I agreed to hold off on discontinuing the steroids until we tried the new drug. For the first time since this puzzling illness began, I felt like I had some control over my life. The drug worked, and I was rapidly weaned from the steroids. My breathing slowly returned to normal, and my body started to rid itself of the devastating toll the effects of the steroids had on me. The decision I made to take control of my life was the beginning of what, I believe, increased my confidence to take on any challenge which came my way.

Soon after, and way before I was ready to get back to living a normal life, I plunged into living life with a vengeance. I went full steam ahead, and as the days passed, and as I got better, I took on arduous projects. I enrolled in a ballet class for people who were aspiring to become professionals to build my physical stamina. I began to learn how to do commercial art (now called graphic design) using a computer because when I was in school graphic design was done entirely by hand. The threat my lungs would stop me from living life as I wanted was always with me propelling me to fill every day with new experiences. It seemed like each accomplishment made me physically and mentally healthier. My near-death experience resulted in an innate willfulness which drove me to take on challenges which intrigued me. Fortunately, my artistic background offered a myriad of options in the art world for me to explore. The children were still young, and my priority was to be an attentive mother and wife, so freelancing, in some artistic endeavor, was a good fit for me. It allowed me the time to be the kind of wife and mother which I aspired to be while taking on new endeavors.

Plunging into the graphic design world was a challenge because I had no previous experience. In those early years, I took on many new projects, learning everything I could about things which interested me. Under the auspices of the company I had created, Held Art and Design, I sought out a variety of freelance opportunities. I designed wrapping paper for the Susan Crane Company, I freelanced as a graphic designer for the Dr Pepper Company, I did advertising design for several catalogs including The Underground Shopper and The Yellow Pages. I became a designer of greeting cards for The Drawing Board Company. I dabbled in interior design and began to build a clientele and become recognized for my ability as an interior designer.

My previous jobs in interior design led me to become interested in designing floral arrangements, and I attempted to register for a class at one of the community colleges. Unfortunately, the course was filled, but I didn't give up. I found out the professor owned a floral shop, so I paid him a visit. He reaffirmed he couldn't add any more students to his class, so I made him an offer he couldn't resist. I offered my free labor in exchange for an apprenticeship at his shop. My proposal was a win for him because he was getting free labor and a win for me to have his undivided tutoring. After I felt I had absorbed all he had to teach me, he hired me. Before long I left the shop to start my own floral design business. The future led me to endless other free-lance endeavors and challenges in which I had no prior experience. My next endeavor was fashion illustration and design.

I had previously designed my own wedding dress, and I was intrigued by the industry. I searched the newspapers and found a local fashion illustrator whose work I admired and contacted her to see if she was willing to teach me her craft. Most people are willing to mentor someone who admires their work. She was willing, and I was then off and running in a new direction.

For me, design influences most aspects of my life. I view life through the lens of design. Whether it is designing a physical object or a program which enhances the world, it influences everything I do.

During those years I also tackled projects which were not art related, but they all took creative thinking to accomplish. While I pursued my career as an artist and designer, I was often diverted by taking on voluntary projects which would make a difference in other's lives. I thrived on the excitement and the adrenaline surge I felt when I tackled projects that took "out of the box thinking" to achieve a positive result.

As I was gaining my reputation in interior design, I volunteered for the Multiple Sclerosis Society where I began by licking envelopes for a fundraising solicitation. Climbing the ranks, I became the Assistant Director in charge of putting on a full-scale rodeo. The organization's yearly major fund-raising event. As far as I knew, in Boston, we didn't have rodeos, so I had never even seen one. Metaphorically, I took the bull by the horns and ran with it. With enough research and imagination, I managed to execute a successful event which brought in more money than the organization had raised in its history.

Shortly after, my son's preschool needed volunteer help at his school and while volunteering I became interested in finding new and innovative ways to teach children. The owners of the school recognized my success in teaching children and asked me to create a Montessori program for the 2-year old siblings of the children who attended the school. Again, I had no related experience, but I taught myself everything I needed to know about the Montessori philosophy and with that framework, created a program geared towards the 2-year olds. I was then hired to be the teacher and proceeded to become the Director of the new preschool program.

My life has been a series of explorations into the unknown which initially seem unattainable. I live by the words of Craig Sager, sportscaster, "Every day is a canvas waiting to be painted." On one particular day, my canvas ended up resembling a Jackson Pollack painting. I was working on a freelance design job for the Dr Pepper company. I was charged with designing the buttons on their vending machines for their new fruit-flavored drinks. My days were often so busy that I would work through the night after the kids went to bed. As the dawn rose, I completed the project which was due that morning. Josh woke up complaining his stomach was hurting, but he didn't have any other symptoms, so I ushered him off to school. I needed him to go to school so I could deliver the completed project. When I got home, Maury called to see if he could bring his new boss home for dinner. Although tired from the night's work, it was important to me to help Maury impress his new boss, so I began planning an elaborate meal. Shortly after, the next call started an avalanche of absurdities challenging my efforts to accomplish an impressive dinner. The school nurse called to let me know Josh was vomiting at school, and I needed to pick him up. On the way to the school, I contemplated the dinner menu and decided to make Veal Marsala.

I picked Josh up, and on the way home stopped for a bottle of marsala wine. At that point, I still had confidence everything was under control. After getting Josh settled, I began feverishly cleaning the house. As I was vacuuming, the cord wrapped around the bottle of red wine flinging it onto the newly painted pastel mauve walls. As I was feverishly trying to clean up the mess which literally looked like a Jackson Pollack painting, the vacuum stopped working. Since I had no sleep the night before, the tension was escalating, but dinner still seemed doable until the day became insane! When Kim came home from school, I sent her next door to borrow a vacuum from the neighbor. Within minutes I heard her screaming from the front yard. She was yelling that she saw a monkey climbing over our fence into the backyard. Surely this could not be happening! I looked out the window into the backyard, and a 6-foot-tall primate was removing the pool equipment off the fence and was proceeding to clean our pool. In utter disbelief, I called 911. To add to the chaos, the police arrived with a cadre of reporters filming this utterly absurd incident. We learned the monkey, named Deana, was trained to entertain at parties and she had escaped from her owner. Apparently, she also was trained to do chores around the house. By 7:00 PM, the pool was cleaned thanks to Deana, and she was returned to her owner. Josh was in bed, dinner was prepared, and Maury arrived home with his boss. As chaotic as the day was, I managed to complete this day's canvas.

The chaos of that day was not a typical day, but often my life was a balancing act with me trying to accomplish all I wanted to do.

My volunteer work, helping people in need, has remained a constant in the balancing of my life. In addition to my innate propensity to help people in need, my Judaism has instilled in me the importance of "tzedakah." The word "tzedakah" is defined as giving aid, assistance, and money to the poor and needy. My empathy for others inspires me to act when I become aware of people who, for one reason or another, have life challenges.

My earliest recollection of my innate empathy was when I was in elementary school. A young child in a wheelchair was playing by the pool at my apartment complex. While all the other children were playing together, she was all alone. My immediate instinct was to play with her as opposed to running with the crowd.

Today we often hear, "If you see something say something" referring to the prevention of the evil occurrences which seem to be happening far too often. For me, before that became a popular slogan, I lived my life by the belief that "If you see something, do something." When I see people in need of help or suffering from something beyond their control, I feel my moral obligation is to try to do something to help them out.

As Kim and Josh were growing up, we became involved in our synagogue, Temple Emanu-El. Maury and I wanted the children to have a rich spiritual experience. The synagogue we joined had a huge congregation. The Rabbi, Elizabeth "Liza" Stern and I became close friends. Few people come along in life who leave an indelible mark, and for me, Liza has been one of those people. Her dependable insight has always been instrumental in helping me to achieve clarity when decisions were complex. She inspired me when doubts threatened my many aspirations, and her mentorship has guided me through good times and tough times. While volunteering my time at the synagogue, Liza and I discussed how hard it was for the Rabbis to find enough time to spend with the numerous hospitalized congregants while fulfilling their other responsibilities. My first thought was I can fix that! The creative part of my brain went to work as I contemplated the problem and came up with a solution. I created a Hospital Visitation Program. I trained 100 volunteers to visit congregants in the local hospitals and report back to the Rabbis. The training that I created taught the volunteers to identify those people who truly needed the attention of a Rabbi and to convey the information back to the Rabbis. I designed a gift bag to be taken to the patients which contained items to celebrate the Sabbath. The kit included details on how to contact the Rabbis if needed. The name of the program was called "Hineni" which is a powerful Hebrew word meaning "Here I am." Ready to help - Ready to reach out. The program became a vehicle for the Rabbi's to be fully informed about hospitalized congregants and attend to those who were in need of a Rabbi. The program succeeded to solve the Rabbis problem and to this day is a valuable component of temple life serving as a support to hospitalized congregants.

While I was implementing the hospital visitation program, I was inspired to start a new business. After designing and implementing a party for 250 people at my daughter's Bat-Mitzvah, word got around, and I became known for my unique execution of party themes and décor of significant events. Again, I was off and running in a new direction.

I never hesitated to do something I knew nothing about. I would get an idea and imagine what the end result would look like when it was successful, and then I would intensely focus on every aspect I needed to know about it to succeed. I would then fearlessly dive in to accomplish what I set out to do. I believe with enough focus on an endeavor, combined with seeking the necessary knowledge, most goals can be achieved. My announcement of "I've got an idea" was often a formidable statement at our house. This usually meant I was about to embark on a new adventure and most times it meant Maury and the kids were also going to be participating in a new experience.

After the Hospital Visitation Program was up and running and my event business was becoming successful, Rabbi Liza asked me if I would participate in a program at Children's Medical Center (CMC) in Dallas to become a hospital chaplain. At the time, there were no Jewish Chaplains in Dallas and only a few in the country. As usual, the prospect of doing something challenging enticed me. This was a far more intense commitment than I anticipated, but as usual, I dove right in. A Chaplain's responsibility is not only to counsel people through tough times but to be by their sides when death knocks on their door, or in this case, their dying child's door. My time at CMC was heartbreaking. Death always seemed to occur at night. As I walked the dark halls, waiting to be called to the bedside for a child's last breath, I would stop to call Maury, and he would always give me the encouragement to face the worst of times. He would reassure me that I knew the right words to ease the pain of these suffering families. If I had a particularly heart-wrenching night, he would come to the "On Call Room" to be with me while I waited to be called for the moment of most profound and darkest sorrow.

My time as a Chaplain at CMC, taught me the importance of being present for someone during the worst of times. Especially during times when death is just moments away, being present, facilitates strangers to communicate in the very most profound way. Death crosses all language barriers and differences between people. Strangers become friends. The loss of every life you touch becomes engraved in one's soul.

While I was fully entrenched in the hospital chaplaincy program, I was still designing and implementing party themes. My business was growing, and my reputation as a designer and implementer of party themes was flourishing. I had an intuitive sense of what people imagined for their décor, and that combined with my artistic eye, enabled me to capture their visions and execute them.

As time went on, the balance between my work as a Chaplain, while simultaneously creating lavish parties, didn't fit together for me. The two parts of my life became diametrically opposed. Part of the time I was organizing these wildly joyous parties, and other times I was counseling families through the hardest times of their lives. The final realization came early one Saturday morning as Maury, Josh, Kim and I were setting up for a large party. We were in the process of constructing a vast balloon arch of all the colors of the rainbow. While we were busy tying the hundreds of knots on the balloons, my thoughts were with a little 9-month-old boy named Ryan whose death was imminent. The pager I was wearing on my belt was the ever-present reminder that Ryan would soon be struggling to take his last breath. I was dreading hearing the inevitable beeps from my pager which would signal me to return to the hospital so I could be there to help the family get through this tragedy. As I waited for the dreaded beep, I realized these two parts of my life could not exist together. At that moment I decided the party business had to stop. Typical of me, I gave up the only thing which was making money to follow my heart instead.

At the height of my success in creating wildly elaborate parties, Maury and I met many people who were designers and artists and creative people in the industry. Many friendships evolved out of these business contacts, and it became apparent that there was something concerning going on in the industry. Increasingly, we were hearing about people in the gay community who had become sick or died from a mysterious disease. As we became more aware of the magnitude of the occurrences, we heard about an organization who was raising money to help those who were afflicted. We were drawn to join the effort to help.

The first organization we joined was called, Design Industries Foundation Fighting AIDS (DIFFA). DIFFA was amongst the early organized efforts in Dallas to be proactive in making a difference in the lives of people with AIDS. The Dallas Chapter of DIFFA, founded in 1984, was and remains, the only HIV/AIDS organization in Texas which funds local service providers. It was the beginning of our involvement in the front lines of the AIDS crisis. As time went on, and we saw the unrelenting disease killing those around us, we became even more involved. We were nominated to the Board of Directors of DIFFA by the Executive Director, Steve Burrus. As we became more involved, we joined Meals on the Move (M.O.M.). A startup effort providing meals to homebound AIDS patients. We also became involved in AIDS Services of Dallas (ASD), an organization in its infancy who was trying to provide housing to people with AIDS who were too debilitated to work. There we met Don Maison, Executive Director, who nominated us to be on the Board. Maury and I each served as Chair of the Board over the years of our service to the organization. As the epidemic raged, we helped out wherever we were needed.

After my chaplaincy internship at CMC, Rabbi Liza asked me to become Director of Pastoral Services at Temple Emanu-El. My position was to assist congregants who were going through difficult times. During my time at the synagogue I developed a bereavement support program and a hot line for congregants needing emergency help. I worked with the Caring Congregation Committee and Social Action Committee to help implement programs which would improve the lives of congregants and the community at large. One of my responsibilities was to be the liaison between the synagogue and community organizations. Because of my previous involvement in AIDS, Rabbi Liza asked me to be the liaison to the AIDS Interfaith Network (AIN). As a result, my participation in caring for people with AIDS became even more intense. I was being drawn even deeper into the world of people with AIDS. What I didn't know at the time, my commitment to helping people with AIDS was about to take over my life.

2

FLASHBACK

As the AIDS epidemic was emerging, I heard whisperings about this strange illness having a life-threatening impact on people. It seemed to have appeared out of nowhere, attacking with unrelenting cruelty. The dark cloud of the disease was drifting across the country and lingering in communities dense with gay men. This merciless virus bludgeoned the lives of those who were affected. Initially, the disease was thought to be exclusively a gay men's plague, but as time progressed, the disease crossed all lines. Under certain circumstances, everyone was at risk of contracting the virus. AIDS was one of the most serious, deadly diseases in human history. Mystery surrounded the contagious nature of the epidemic and terror reigned throughout society because the medical community could not come up with any answers. People contracting the disease were shunned and isolated while they were trying to survive an illness nobody knew how to treat. As I observed this atrocious epidemic creeping into the lives of so many, I was compelled to help those who contracted this ruthless illness. Drawn to helping the alienated and suffering, this was the first time a scandal-plagued epidemic gripped my soul and set me on a journey which would have an all-consuming impact on my family and me.

Around 1980, AIDS became more widely known, as a life-threatening disease lurking in the shadows of our country. People were getting sick, and nobody knew why or how. They began dying long before it even had a name. Initially, the only concrete publicly known fact, was a strange illness was killing primarily gay men. The fatal disease was spreading rapidly, ravaging men's bodies and killing them swiftly. Early on, the illness was called the Gay Men's Cancer, and some referred to it as Gay-related Immune Deficiency. Death loomed over the gay community and doctors had no explanations, only a storm of questions.

In many instances, throughout history, gay men were forced to live in a behind-the-scenes subculture, routinely subjected to harassment and persecution. Throughout their lives, gay people often became the target of horrendous violent acts. Stigma and fear of rejection often forced them to hide their true identity from their families and acquaintances. For some, suicide became the only alternative to the pain they suffered from the persecution. A theory that existed, which is now not accepted by most people, was that being gay was a misguided choice which could be altered with conversion therapy or brainwashing. In 1952 The American Psychiatric Association perpetuated the belief in this theory by classifying homosexuality as a mental disorder, erroneously validating those who believed it could be cured. In 1953, President Dwight D. Eisenhower signed an executive order banning homosexuals from working in the federal government, demeaning the gay community further. As prejudice prevailed, even as recent as 1993, President Bill Clinton signed a military policy prohibiting openly gay and lesbian Americans from serving in the military, implying their mere presence was a threat to others. For a long time, gay people had no civil rights protections and were treated as if they were a less valuable community. Today the American Psychiatric Association and the American Medical Association has warned against the use of conversion therapy because of the destructive effect it has had on so many who were conflicted throughout their lives. Some states now have banned the use of this therapy by licensed therapists. It was a long bumpy road before any change occurred and then to complicate matters this mysterious, life-threatening disease rained down like a blight on the gay community intensifying prejudice and fear.

By organizing and forcibly speaking out, the gay rights movement towards equality has made massive progress in the last two decades. The gay community has made great strides in demanding equal rights, but as with many minority populations, there is still a long way to go for total acceptance without prejudice.

When HIV/AIDS struck, the gay community already had achieved organizational abilities during their fight for equality which became invaluable during the epidemic. The gay community vocally forced society to recognize this killer disease. They came together and demanded attention be focused on the epidemic which was killing their community. They formed organizations which took care of the sick. They raised money to provide services, fund research and explore effective treatments, long before our government became actively engaged.

Over time there have been many theories about the origin of the disease in the United States. Initially, researchers concluded a sexually prolific male flight attendant carried the virus from Europe to New York. There are many diverse opinions about how he originally contracted it. The theory that the flight attendant was patient zero has always been disputed. Currently, the consensus is it initially came from the blood of an infected primate in Cameroon, Africa. Some believe, a hunter killed a chimp who had the virus and then had contact with the blood of the dead animal, transferring the disease from the chimp to the hunter. After the disease mutated slightly, it then began to be passed from one person to another through bodily fluids. How the disease got from the hunter in Africa to someone in New York is still not known.

In October 2016, NBC News reported on a new genetic study conducted by researcher Michael Worobey. The report stated the epidemic showed up in this country in New York around 1970. His findings suggested the outbreak moved from New York to San Francisco in about 1976. Worobey stated, "In New York City, the virus encountered a population that was like dry tinder, causing the epidemic to burn hotter and faster and infecting enough people that it grabbed the world's attention for the first time."

Contrary to the wide spread belief that the epidemic began in the 1980s, researchers now conclude, people with similar symptoms, were dying from the disease as early as the 1970s. Researchers eventually ascertained, through DNA testing of blood samples collected a decade earlier, people with a particular combination of symptoms, had been dying in this country a lot longer than initially thought.

Even before this dark shadow enveloped the gay community, gay people were a mistreated and oppressed minority. Just as their fight for recognition and inclusion began to make headway, the virus began infecting the population. Alienation prevailed once again. Society became afraid of being around people who were gay for fear they might be carrying the disease. No one knew exactly how it was transmitted, and the medical community was just as uncertain as everyone else. Fear of contracting the disease was the catalyst for provoking a flood of questions from the alarmed. Was it airborne? Were surfaces contaminated? Could one get it from their gay hairdresser? Was the virus in saliva? Could one catch it from sharing food with someone who was infected? Could it be spread from kissing, touching or even shaking hands with someone who had the disease? Questions and rumors flourished throughout society in an uncontrolled flurry of fear.

Finally, the deadly virus was identified as the Human Immunodeficiency Virus (HIV). As the virus progresses and a person begins to have opportunistic infections they are referred to as having Acquired Immune Deficiency Syndrome (AIDS). In the initial HIV stages, a person who was carrying the virus could go for years unaware he had contracted it, which contributed to the uncontrolled spread of the disease.

At the onset of the disease, HIV can resemble flu-like symptoms which occur 2 to 4 weeks after contracting the virus. However, some people do not always recognize or get flu-like symptoms. This stage of the disease called the "clinical latency stage," can last decades. In many instances, during this stage, the condition can go undiagnosed. The final stage, when the patient is contracting opportunistic infections and exhibiting visible symptoms, the disease is referred to as full-blown AIDS.

HIV destroys cells which are critical to a healthy immune system. Those cells, called CD4, more commonly known as T cells, are white blood cells which fight infection. The higher the number of T cells, the better a person can fight off diseases which are trying to attack the body. As time goes on and the number of these fighter cells decline, the disease develops into AIDS. AIDS is diagnosed when HIV has weakened the immune system enough that the body has difficulty fighting viruses and infections.

In some instances, many years can go by while the disease is silently affecting the immune system. During that time, it is likely the virus is being passed from one person to another accounting for the rapid spread of the disease. Often not until the disease has progressed and symptoms become apparent, do doctors realize the particular symptoms might indicate the person should be tested for HIV. The diagnosis of a positive HIV test raises more questions than answers in the newly diagnosed.

When the disease progresses to full-blown AIDS, the physical manifestations are so apparent that it contributes to the isolation of these ill people. As the virus progresses and the infected person's immune system deteriorates, the patient begins to face life-altering symptoms. Particular opportunistic infections such as Kaposi's Sarcoma, causing cancerous skin lesions, a specific type of pneumonia called Pneumocystis Carinii, and Wasting Syndrome which causes rapid weight loss, are often common signs of the disease's progression.

Ultimately, a once healthy person becomes bed-ridden, extremely gaunt, and suffers from a combination of infections which can repeatedly attack every part of the body. At the end of their life, shriveled bodies, marred with oozing sores, lay waiting for death to come and often hoping it would happen soon.

From the beginning, the disease started spreading like wildfire. Before the various modes of transmission were identified, the gay community lived in fear of contracting the disease. As women and children began to be diagnosed with the disease, it became even more puzzling, and everyone felt vulnerable.

The Center for Disease Control (CDC) eventually established the disease was being spread by the exchange of bodily fluids between people. Blood, semen, vaginal fluids and breastmilk were likely vehicles which were transferring the virus from one person to another.

In addition to sexual activity in the gay community, IV drug users who were sharing needles with the infected were also at an increased risk of contracting the disease. Women were contracting it through blood transfusions, sexual activity with an infected partner or their own IV drug use. Infected pregnant women were passing the disease to their unborn children. Anyone requiring blood transfusions were also vulnerable. Hemophiliacs, who were dependent on frequent transfusions of blood products to treat their condition, were at highly increased risk.

The diagnosis of the disease in women and children was slow to be recognized by doctors because the medical community was initially considering the disease to be a gay men's illness. In families, most often a positive diagnosis of one member also raised the possibility that additional family members could be infected. Infected families were driven into isolation because unlike the support the gay community had already organized, there was not a support system targeted to the different kinds of needs families and children had.

In 1981, women accounted for 8% of new infections. New infections rose sharply among women during the first decade of the epidemic. In 1983, doctors began recognizing infants were also acquiring HIV perinatally from their infected mothers during pregnancy and during the birth process. Perinatal transmission was the primary cause of the virus in newborns. This phenomenon increased dramatically over the decade, with the transmission of the virus from an infected mother to her newborn occurring 30% to 60% of the time. Sometimes it took up to 2 years of age to confirm whether the newborn who initially tested positive was truly infected. Unlike adults who may remain asymptomatic for eight years or more, children often display symptoms within the first two years of life. Some of the infants converted to HIV negative during that time and remained negative. However, there were a few reports that later in life some children reverted to being HIV positive. Initially, it was predicted that most infants born with HIV/AIDS, who were truly infected, were not expected to live more than nine months. Within 2 years of diagnosis, the average pediatric mortality rate was 80%.

Children who had various other medical problems requiring transfusions of blood products were also at an increased risk of contracting HIV. A child with the virus often went undiagnosed until the child was gravely ill. At the onset of the epidemic, identifying the disease in children was problematic for several reasons: Most pediatricians had very little, or no experience with this disease. Also, doctors would not suspect the child had the virus because of its relative rarity in children. Most often, the disease was not suspected in a newborn whose mother did not know she was carrying the disease. Symptoms of the disease in children are also different than in adults, making the diagnosis even more challenging. Signs of the disease in a child often resembled common childhood illnesses. The alarming recurrence of bacterial infections, strep throat and meningitis, repeated bouts of pneumonia and an overall failure to thrive were the most common clues. To make a correct diagnosis and conclude that the underlying cause of the illnesses was HIV, took mystified diagnosticians time and in some cases the diagnosis came too late. For a variety of these reasons, a child could be very ill and die without ever having been diagnosed with AIDS.

Those early years were justifiably frightening. Mounting a response to figure out the answers was slow in coming because of the lack of government funding. Once the disease was identified, and the mode of transmission was uncovered, finding a treatment became the challenge. Once treatment was discovered, the drug was put on a fast track for approval, but it was still a long time for those who were suffering to get some relief. Not until March 19, 1987, did Azidothymidine (AZT), initially the only drug approved to treat the disease, became available by prescription. The drug came with many toxic side effects which sometimes caused additional unbearable symptoms. AZT was the only treatment available which could potentially minimize the manifestations of the disease and in some cases possibly extend life, but it was not a cure.

Many medical professionals were afraid to take care of the sick and dying. They felt they were putting themselves at risk of contracting the disease when treating people with the virus. Some even denied treating the infected. Critical surgeries, which patients needed because of the effects of the disease, were denied. Hospitals isolated patients with AIDS, plastering large caution signs on the doors to their rooms much like a crime scene. A plentiful supply of gowns, gloves, and masks were piled up outside the hospital room doors, warning all who entered their own life might be at risk. People with AIDS were isolated and made to feel like lepers while they suffered.

When death finally came, cemeteries often refused to accept the bodies, morticians refused to prepare the bodies for burial, and the clergy would not perform the funerals. Many of the deceased were already alienated from their families because they disapproved of the person's lifestyle, and in some instances, relatives of the deceased wanted nothing to do with the remains. Due to prejudice and persecution, many gay people did not reveal their gender preference to their families and as a result their parents first learned they were gay when they were notified that their child had passed away from AIDS.

In the early days of the epidemic, most people turned away from people with the disease, but Maury and I turned towards them. We reached out to the gay Jewish congregation, Beth El Binah, because we had friends in the group and wanted to provide support to their members who were suffering from the disease. When the inevitable first death happened to a member, we knew finding someone to officiate at the funeral would be a challenge. During the height of the AIDS crisis many religious leaders, of all denominations, feared having contact with anyone who had the disease, even when they had already passed away. Also, many had profoundly ingrained prejudice against a person being gay. I began to search for anyone who would be willing to perform the service. I didn't have to look too far because my friend and mentor, Rabbi Liza, when asked, did not hesitate to consent to officiate at the funeral.

I observed something surprising which seemed to be going on in the midst of the crisis. In spite of all the sorrow surrounding this epidemic, some people began slowly, very slowly, to gain some compassion for gay people. The gay community could not be ignored as easily as in past history because of how prominent the AIDS crisis was. I first noticed this phenomenon in my own congregation Temple Emanu-El: Beth El Binah became welcomed into the mainstream of the synagogue's congregation. I'm not naive in thinking this was a prevalent feeling among most people. However, a little glimmer of acceptance of gay people by those who had previously been prejudice began to emerge. People who were innately compassionate were gaining awareness of the gay plight, and some took action to be supportive.

It was a tragic time in our nation and around the world. Many were suffering from this daunting epidemic. The more prevalent it became; the more determined Maury and I were to help. Our willingness to help became our mission.

Maury and I were often asked why we became involved in the AIDS crisis. People would automatically assume we had someone close to us with the disease and they were surprised to hear we did not. The answer was simple: in this tragic time in United States history, people were suffering, and we could not turn a blind eye.

Many people did not always revere our involvement in the epidemic. Some feared because of our association with people with AIDS we might be carrying the disease ourselves. In the beginning, even the supposedly well-informed, were fraught with fear and ignorance about how the virus was being transmitted.

One night at a dinner event, we were seated beside a doctor and his wife. The conversation eventually evolved into the AIDS crisis and our involvement. Before very long, they made some feigned excuse and moved to another table.

There were also some people who were in denial about the epidemic actually existing. Maury and I had become so involved in the epidemic we would be shocked when we encountered people who were completely unaware the epidemic was going on.

Maury and I chose compassion over fear. Many tried to discourage us from taking care of the sick and dying. We were accused of being careless with our own lives, and some people tried to convince us we were even putting our own children's lives at risk. However, what we did know at the time, if we used proper precautions, AIDS was not a threat to us or our family. We were reassured by medical professionals that standard safety precautions, used to prevent contracting any virus, would protect us when we were having physical contact with someone who was infected. Initially, the Center for Disease Control (CDC) recommended gloves, masks, and gowns be worn while having contact with an infected person. Fortunately, as time went on and knowledge was acquired, these precautions became unnecessary in situations where bodily fluids were not being exchanged.

In an interview, which Maury and I gave to the Texas Women's News, Maury was asked if he was afraid of being around people who were infected. His answer was "Yes, I was concerned. I was scared of it. I knew if I did get it and died, I'd die knowing I did the right thing, and I know Stefanie believes that also."

3

COMPELLED BY COMPASSION

In the mid-1980s, during the time Maury and I were deeply involved in the gay men's AIDS crisis, Rabbi Liza contacted me to tell me about a family who needed help. The only information we had was the family, Lydia, Scott and their two children, Matthew and Bryan, were infected with the virus. Liza said they were moving to Dallas from Colorado Springs because they had become ostracized from their community.

Until that point, we had not had any contact or much awareness of families with HIV/AIDS. Not knowing much else about the family, I told Rabbi Liza I would like to have them over for dinner when they arrived in Dallas. I assumed this family must be devastated and experiencing the kind of anguish that thankfully most of us could never imagine. Doing something to help, and not turning away as most in society was inclined to do back then, was important to us.

Rabbi Liza contacted them and extended my invitation for them to come to dinner. The dinner was planned for Sunday, July 5, 1987. That day turned out to be a brutally hot day in Dallas. The sun was beating down and wilting everything it touched, including me. While I was preparing the meal, the outside temperature was hovering around 100 degrees. Keeping the kitchen cool enough while I was cooking in the sweltering heat was difficult. The oven I was using to prepare the meal vastly contributed to the temperature in the kitchen, and I was hoping I could finish in time to shower the day's heat off me before our guests arrived. I had spent hours in the kitchen preparing a gourmet dinner for our guests. When I finished making the meal, I had just enough time for the shower which was beckoning me. As I was lavishing in the cool water, I began to feel somewhat uneasy. Compassion and concern began to take over my thoughts - compassion for these strangers who carried this mysterious disease and concern that our backgrounds were very different. I wondered whether we would have anything in common with these strangers. I was somewhat apprehensive about four people from different worlds being comfortable with each other. I suspected we had more differences than similarities. Their background was distinctly different from ours. We were a Jewish family and not very conservative. Scott was a conservative minister. His wife, Lydia, was a nurse and I assumed, as a minister's wife, she led a very different life from mine. I had many questions darting through my head. Were these people open to accepting us and who we were? Did I need to fear the health risks which still weren't very clear? Was I jeopardizing my family's health? Did we have anything in common?

Maury had an extraordinary ability to communicate with people, and I had confidence, that his ever-present charm, would at least be able to keep the conversation going. Also, I had faith our open hearts, open minds and open arms could overcome any differences we had.

When they arrived for dinner, Lydia was barely able to hold her head up. She was about my height, 5'1", but very thin and frail. The dark circles under her eyes looked like pools of sadness. She appeared weak and pale. At the time, there was no effective medication to ease the effects of the virus, and she was quite ill. The misery which she had been going through, since the family's diagnosis of AIDS, enveloped her physical appearance.

Dinner was carefully planned to consider the uncertainty about the risks of transmission of the disease which was still being questioned by some. I was not wary of casual contact, but I had concerns about being careless about the unknown risk factors of sharing food and utensils. I consciously chose a menu calculated to serve separate portions. We sat on the sofa chatting and sharing a dip I had prepared while we got acquainted. As we sat there talking and getting to know each other, it suddenly occurred to me, I neglected to think about sharing the dip! It was just a fleeting thought because from all I did know sharing food was not a vehicle for transmission, but with the definitive unknowns lurking, I couldn't help giving it a thought.

Dinner was a rapid initiation into a strong friendship. We joined our lives in an unlikely relationship of four strangers. This family's plight deeply touched our souls, and before they left our house, without speaking to each other, Maury and I knew, we were committed to doing whatever we could to help this family. The next time we got together, Maury presented Lydia with a T-shirt he ordered which had the words printed on it which said, "Life may not be the party we asked for, but as long as we are here, we should dance."

During that first dinner, they told us their tragic story. Lydia and Scott were living in San Francisco in 1982, a major hub of the AIDS virus at the time. Lydia was pregnant with their first child, and when the time came to give birth, she and her newborn had a complicated delivery. During the birth, she required lifesaving transfusions of blood platelets to keep her and her baby alive. Lydia gave birth to a baby boy, and they named him Matthew. At the time, no one suspected the transfusion she received was tainted with a deadly virus. During the birth process, the tainted blood had the opportunity to circulate through Lydia and her newborn son Matthew's body. It was never confirmed whether he became HIV positive during the birth process or through breastfeeding. There was no way to know absolutely.

Scott, Lydia, and their first child Matthew then moved to Colorado Springs from San Francisco for Scott's ministry in 1984. Not knowing she and Matthew were carrying HIV, Lydia became pregnant again and gave birth to a second child who they named Bryan. He was born three months premature in May of 1985. Bryan spent much of his little life with unexplained reoccurring illnesses from the time of his birth. Doctors were mystified about his constant illnesses and did not initially have the answer to why this little boy was so ill.

Several months after Bryan was born Scott and Lydia were notified by the blood bank in San Francisco that the transfusion which Lydia received, while giving birth to her first child Matthew, contained the AIDS virus.

After testing the whole family, they learned the devastating news that Lydia, Scott, Matthew, and Bryan were all HIV positive. Not until sometime later did Scott learn his test had been mixed up with someone else's and he was not HIV positive. Scott was the only one in the family who managed to escape the ravages of the disease, but he did not escape the wrath. The expectations of their life together disintegrated instantaneously. Scott's whole family had been given a death sentence.

Scott informed the church where he was a minister, and members immediately asked for his resignation. He was told not to return to the church, and they would send him his personal belongings. Lydia was forced to take Matthew out of the church's daycare, and the family was asked not to return to church. Lydia became terrified she and her children would become victims of the persecution which she had seen in the media. Lydia pulled down the blinds of their home and cared for her gravely ill infant. After learning their secret was traveling through the town where they lived, they decided to leave.

In the dark of night, with a critically ill infant, who had little chance of surviving the trip, Lydia and baby Bryan set out on the long drive. They headed to Fort Worth, Texas where Scott's family lived. Their hope was they could be anonymous and get the support they needed. Scott and Matt flew, but Lydia and Bryan had to drive because the airlines would not transport a critically ill child and the medical equipment which he needed. With instructions from Bryan's doctor, if he died during the trip, she was to continue on to Fort Worth. Bryan died at nine months old on February 2, 1986. Bryan was the first child recognized to die of perinatally acquired AIDS in the Dallas/Fort Worth area.

Scott and Lydia made every effort to protect the family's anonymity because this was a very frightening time for people surrounding the HIV/AIDS crisis. In the beginning, the lack of definitive information from the medical community had everyone on edge. Even as the facts became known, they were slow to be believed. Ignorance and persecution prevailed. The constant flow of horrific stories of harassment towards people with AIDS was ongoing in the news.

Scott and Lydia's concerns were justified because a plethora of media coverage highlighted the fear of HIV/AIDS. Two prominent stories which were repeatedly making headlines during those early years of the epidemic were about the persecution being endured by two families with young boys who were infected: Ryan White and the Ray brothers.

Sometime between the late 1970s and early 1980s, Ryan White, a child with Hemophilia, received a transfusion of blood products containing the virus. To treat his Hemophilia, Ryan had received multiple transfusions of blood products to stay alive. On December 17, 1984, Ryan was diagnosed with AIDS and given 6 months to live. He was one of the first children with Hemophilia to be identified with AIDS. Ryan and his family lived in Indiana, but they gained national attention because of Ryan's brave fight to be allowed to go to school. He was ostracized, accused of being gay, and was repeatedly told he must have done something wrong to have contracted AIDS. Ryan's family became the target of torment. Vandals broke windows at their home, and the community would not have any contact with Ryan or his family. Through his perseverance, he won his brave fight to be allowed to go to school. He said, "he just wanted to be a regular kid." He died one month before he graduated high school in April of 1990 at 18 years old.

The persecution of people with HIV/AIDS continued and in the early '90s, the Ray family in Arcadia, Florida, had three young boys with Hemophilia. They learned Ricky, Robert and Randy ages 10, 9, and 8 were all infected with HIV. The media widely covered their story. The family was continuously threatened by the people who lived in their community. They lived in constant peril. They received bomb threats and multiple abusive calls at their home, and the school they attended was besieged with threats. Ultimately, their house was burned to the ground.

These and many of the other publicized stories of persecution forced Scott and Lydia to hide their families secret from everyone.

4

LIVES IN CRISIS

As I got more entrenched in the lives of people living with HIV/AIDS, I observed the gay community taking a proactive stance to form a support system around the infected. They were at the forefront of establishing community-based services to assist people who were infected with the disease. They created organizations providing resources for case management, assistance to the homebound, free housing, counseling, and testing centers. The services were tailored to meet the needs of single males. Being in the minority, the focus was not on the needs of women and children with the disease; therefore, families were on their own to try to find the support they needed. Women and their families lived secluded, suffering in silence, and in desperate need of assistance.

In Dallas, an organization providing pastoral care was formed to augment the services the gay community had already established. The pastoral care program was based out of St. Thomas Episcopal Church, a small church with a liberal, compassionate priest, Father Ted Karpf. The church had a diverse congregation which was located not too far from the Oaklawn area of Dallas, a primarily gay residential and entertainment area. The congregation had a sizable number of gay members because of its location. Father Ted began seeing that the gay men in his congregation were getting sick and dying in alarming numbers. They were all dying from what was just starting to be recognized as AIDS. Father Ted joined the effort of the gay community and formed the AIDS Interfaith Network (AIN).

As Director of Pastoral Services at Temple Emanu-El, I became a representative for the synagogue on the board of AIN. AIN is a multi-denominational organization which provides pastoral care and comfort to people with HIV/AIDS. The board was made up of concerned religious leaders in the community. The mission of these leaders was to educate their congregants to the plight of people with HIV/AIDS and to create ministries which would come to the aid of people with the disease. They were also charged with enlisting other religious leaders in the community, who were resistant to ministering to people with the disease. In the beginning, their focus was mainly on men with the disease. Not until the mid-1980s, did AIN become aware of the growing number of women, children and entire families who were also being affected. They concluded their mission should include this newly recognized population and extend their commitment to families with AIDS. Until then, children and families were left to endure the disease in isolation.

AIN formed a woman with AIDS support group with the intention of facilitating socialization for affected women. A venue where these women could get together in a nonjudgmental environment. A place where they could help and support each other. I offered space for them to meet weekly at Temple Emanu-El. Our meetings were secretive. The gatherings felt like a clandestine operation. The women were afraid for anyone to know they were attending a woman with AIDS support group and I had to protect their anonymity. I also had to keep them out of sight of the congregation to protect them from people who might object to their presence.

The support group became a lifeline for these women. The group began with less than a handful of women, their children, and a facilitator. The women were all infected except for one who was a grandmother and the primary caretaker of her infected granddaughter. Some of their children were in various stages of the disease, and some were uninfected. At the first meeting, I asked the group if I could sit in on the sessions, so I could learn more about the plight of families dealing with the virus. I became a weekly participant in the group and sometimes a facilitator when the facilitator was not available. Week after week, the exchange of conversation among the infected women tore at my heartstrings. I became intimately aware of how these women were struggling through this tragic diagnosis. The problems seemed insurmountable, and their resources were nonexistent. I began helping them in any way I could. I gathered donations of money and essential goods and provided transportation to medical appointments and I took care of their children when needed.

What I was doing was not enough; they needed so much more. I couldn't stop thinking about what else I could do to help. Intuitively I knew this was just the beginning of the avalanche of women who were hiding in the shadows of the epidemic. I was sure when word got out about the support group, women would be drawn to the only help available to them. I knew I needed to come up with a plan to help them, but I wasn't sure what the plan would be.

Four women arrived at the first meeting, each with her own unique heartbreaking stories. Three were Caucasians, and one was African American. Three of the women were married to uninfected men and one woman was not married. Two of the women had HIV positive children, and two had children with full-blown AIDS. One woman had two uninfected children from a previous marriage.

The women and their children entered through a side door at the synagogue, so they wouldn't be noticed. Their widespread fear their anonymity might be compromised was a constant in each of their lives. They and their families had all been living a life of isolation, fearing somebody would find out they and their families were infected with HIV/AIDS. They were all living with the possibility that persecution could reign down on their lives at any time. All the women had their children with them because they were not able to get childcare for their sick or even their uninfected children because of the stigma and fear prevalent in society. Each one of the women had an aura of sadness consuming her appearance and some appeared very ill.

We met in the basement of the synagogue where they would be least likely to be seen. The room we met in was previously used to store unused furniture. The room had dim lighting and smelled dank. There was an overall feeling of darkness which seemed to reflect the overall atmosphere looming over the lives of these women. We sat in a circle, on tiny child-size wooden chairs which had been borrowed from the preschool.

Each woman finally felt free to talk about her tragic existence and to exchange ideas which might solve their many problems.

For some, these meetings were the first opportunity to talk about what was going on in their life. No one judged anyone in the room. There was only compassion for one another. They poured their hearts out with uncontrolled eagerness. I sat silently, listening to what they were going through. All I could think about was what could I do to help.

Off to the side, the children played together. These kids were also living isolated lives without playmates because of a disease which was thrust upon them. In contrast to the sadness of the women, the children smiled and giggled as they played. Unlike their parents, they were fortunate to be unaware of the circumstances which had taken over their lives.

Lydia and Matthew were in the support group along with Linda and her three children, Marilyn and her son Alex, (Linda and Marilyn's names are changed to protect their anonymity), Dorothy and her granddaughter Lindsay.

I met Lindsay and her grandmother Dorothy when Lindsay was a little under two years old. Dorothy was a dedicated mother of nine successful children, and she had one daughter who had problems with drug addiction. When her drug-dependent daughter became pregnant, Dorothy quit her job as a chef, so she would be able to care for her daughter. When her daughter gave birth, Dorothy cared for the infant until one of her other daughters took over the care of the baby, so Dorothy could go back to work. Shortly after, the baby Lindsay got very ill. After some time, doctors discovered baby Lindsay and her mother had AIDS. The baby was given nine months to live. With enormous sacrifice to come, Dorothy committed to taking over the care of the baby until the end. Fearing persecution, she confined herself and Lindsay to a life of isolation. Dorothy kept Lindsay's disease a secret, but eventually, word got out. Although Dorothy took extreme precautions to protect everyone from the risk of contact with Lindsay's bodily fluids, her family would not come around anymore. Her pastor would not allow Dorothy and Lindsay to go to church. Trash collectors were fearful and would not take her garbage away. Even her husband was frightened to have physical contact with Dorothy and Lindsay. Dorothy was forced to sell off all her possessions, so she and Lindsay could have enough money to survive. Dorothy was determined to keep Lindsay healthy and to defy the death sentence she had been given. When she arrived at the support group, her most immediate need at the time, aside from understanding companionship, was for a vast amount of diapers to keep Lindsay free of infection from possible life-threatening diaper rash. With little effort on my part, I began collecting money and diapers from everyone I knew. It was becoming clear to me I could make a difference in the lives of these women and children.

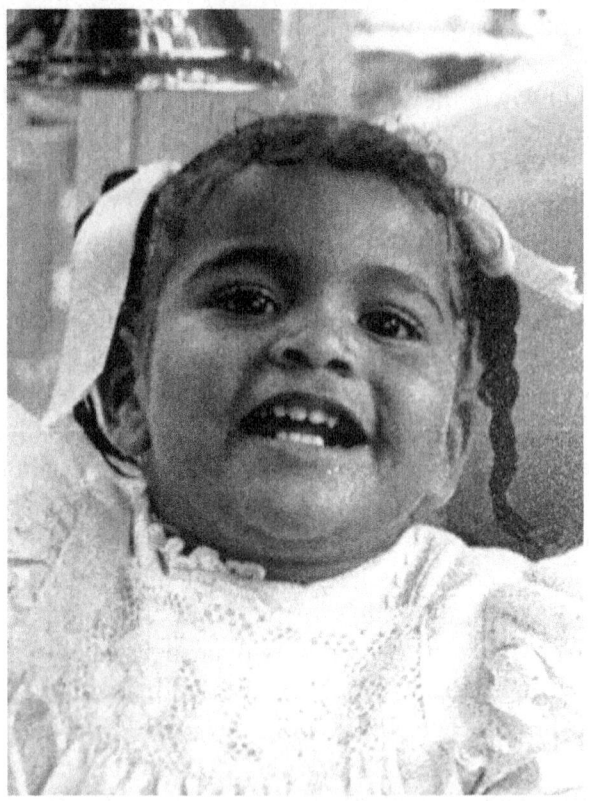

Lindsay Cushingberry

Marylin, a 20-year-old woman with a history of Epilepsy and mental disabilities became pregnant and planned to give up her baby when she gave birth. She had been living in a home for unwed mothers while she was pregnant. During one of her prenatal visits, she was informed she had AIDS. Prior to becoming pregnant, she was uneducated, homeless, and alienated from her family. When the administrators of the home found out she was infected, she was promptly evicted from the facility and informed they would not place her baby up for adoption because no one would take a baby who was born HIV positive. She was cast out on the street, pregnant and living with a secret which she had to hide from the world. She roamed from shelter to shelter until her baby was born. When she gave birth, she became a single mother, alone without anyone to offer her support or assistance. She was ill-equipped for parenthood, lacking instincts or skills to care for an infant, especially one with potential medical needs. Desperate to support herself and her baby, she took a job in a "Gentleman's Club" as a topless waitress. When she and her baby, Alex, joined the support group, she was not sure whether her tiny son was truly infected, or he was only testing positive because the test reflected her immune system.

As I became more involved with these women, I told them I was willing and able to be there for them when they needed help. Shortly after the group formed, Marylin reached out to me in an emergency.

My phone rang one night about 2:00 AM. When I answered, a panicked voice said, "I stabbed my breast with a corkscrew last night opening a bottle of wine for a customer, and I think it's infected. I have red streaks from my nipple to my shoulder. "I need help and don't have anyone else to turn to."

Although she didn't identify herself, I recognized Marylin's voice. I said "I'm on my way. Pack up the baby." Maury and I immediately threw on clothes and headed her way.

When Maury and I arrived at her apartment, neither of us thought about the danger of entering this dark and run-down apartment complex. We were just focused on rescuing this woman and her baby. Marylin was standing on the curb holding a light blue baby blanket and an empty infant seat. She was shivering from the combination of fever and the cold night air.

I asked her "Where's Alex?" She then told me "When I was bringing Alex's things to the curb, the door shut behind me, and I forgot to take my keys." Alex was locked inside her apartment all alone.

I asked her "Is there an onsite manager?" It should have been evident to me that her apartment complex, which was in total disrepair, wasn't the type of place which would have 24-hour management.

She then told me "No, but I think there is a person in the next building who might have a key."

I peered through the window, and I could see the baby was sleeping on the floor. I contemplated breaking the window, so I could open the door, but then decided he looked safe for the moment. At that point, we needed to quickly retrieve the key. Luckily the neighbor did have a key. We retrieved the key and went in and got the baby. After taking her to the emergency room, we took the baby home with us. The next day I took Alex to work with me at the synagogue. I kept the door to my office shut hoping no one would notice I had an HIV positive baby with me. I was somewhat concerned that people who were not privy to me conducting a support group for people with AIDS at the temple that it might jeopardize my use of the space for the group. Fortunately, my fears were not realized.

When Linda joined the group, she was a mother of three children. She became aware she was infected when she was 28. Her frail appearance epitomized the reality of AIDS. When I met her, she was 5 feet 8 inches tall and weighed 99 pounds and was visibly very ill. Early on in Linda's life, she had been married and divorced and became a single mother of two children. While she was a single mom, she dated a variety of men. She eventually became engaged to an attorney who she had been dating for seven months. In the heat of an argument, when their relationship was coming to an end, he confessed he had bisexual experiences before their relationship. Two years after they parted, he found out he had

AIDS and contacted Linda to tell her. At that time, few people had any knowledge about the disease or the heightened risks of contracting the disease by having bisexual relationships. About a year after she broke up with the attorney, Linda met and married her second husband. Not knowing she had become HIV positive, she became pregnant. In the sixth month of her pregnancy, she became ill and was diagnosed with HIV. She believed she contracted the virus from the attorney she was engaged to. As all infants born to infected mothers, her baby was born HIV positive. Before the support group began, Linda came down with Pneumocystis Carinii Pneumonia. The type of pneumonia which often is one of the first signs of the dreaded disease's progress. When Linda joined the group, she had full-blown AIDS. She had been living in isolation battling the effects of the disease while trying to maintain the care of her children. The support group became her lifeline. In one of our many conversations, Linda, weakened by the various opportunistic infections which accompany the virus said, "The most difficult part of the disease is that it has made me almost incapable of caring for my children."

Linda declined rapidly. She was clearly in the latter stages of the disease, and the inevitability of death seemed like it was not in the very distant future. Wearing the mandatory gloves, gown, and mask I sat holding her hand during her last hospitalization. Linda's life was drifting from her body. As she went in and out of consciousness, she had brief moments of clarity. Her faint voice mainly uttered concerns for her children. As she got closer to death, it felt like the light in the room was slowly dimming. Through intermittent gasps for breath, her last audible words to me were "I'm not afraid of dying (gasp) I'm only worried about my children (gasp) and who will take care of them when I die."

I said, "I will."

Linda was the first to die in the support group. My commitment to her was not just a conciliatory statement I made to a dying woman, but it was an intense motivator that inspired me to take action to somehow help these women and their children that were left behind. My compassion inspired me to make it my mission. From that time on, almost all my thoughts revolved around figuring out a solution for the children who were left behind and the families who were suffering through this terrible predicament. I knew, as the numbers of these families were increasing, just my assistance to families like hers, was not enough. My innate compassion kept tugging at me. I had no doubt, one way or another, I could make a significant difference in the lives of these suffering souls. My commitment to come up with a solution was dependent on figuring out what these families needed and what I needed to put in place to help them during this tragedy. Obviously, I couldn't do anything about the underlying AIDS, but what I could do, was to figure something out which could make the lives of these families and children somewhat less difficult while they were enduring this nightmare. The women needed so many different kinds of help during the various stages of the disease. Being gravely ill themselves, many were also taking care of an infected husband and possibly infected children. A solution was needed for a continuum of care for the families and the abandoned children who were left to live out their lives in hospitals.

These women were just the first to join the support group, but many more came when word got out that there was help available. Women began emerging from their isolation. Each new person who joined had her own tragic story about how she got infected. Each one was struggling to maintain her life as the cruel disease tore their life apart. These women found themselves in a predicament few could imagine. They were suddenly presented with a nightmarish diagnosis which was going to make them go through intense suffering and would inevitably end in death. For many, their devastation was compounded by the unthinkable fact that their spouse or child was also enduring the same atrocious suffering. Few things are harder than an ill parent trying to take care of an ill child or an ill spouse or sometimes multiple ill family members. The disease often rendered a parent incapable of doing routine chores which most well people do daily. For years there was not any treatment to ease the suffering. All anyone could do to help was to make day-to-day living a little easier for the infected. People usually rally around ill people and offer help, but with AIDS it was quite the opposite. In many instances, the unfortunate families were alienated from their friends and extended family and had no one willing to help them.

The type of support each woman in the group had varied, but they all needed help, and compassion while enduring the complexities of the disease. Some just needed to be with people who understood what they were going through and not judge them as many in society at large were doing, and some required intensive care. Most had many needs which were seemingly insurmountable from their perspective.

In many instances, the toll of coping with the disease tore families apart. Much like any family tragedy, relationships were being torn apart because they could not withstand the stress of the circumstances. Trying to cope with a death sentence impacting every aspect of their life, often resulted in the relationship dissolving, leaving an infected person and possibly children to endure the manifestations of their illness alone.

The problems which ensued, from having this disease, were multi-faceted, some physical and some emotional. Many had complex medical problems which were painful and debilitating. They were gravely ill and suffering while enduring the ultimate pain of watching the people they loved die one by one.

Often the person who was left behind was also infected and in many instances were unwilling or incapable of caring for an HIV infected child. The children that were affected had few options when both parents died. Relatives were often reluctant to care for the children because of the stigma and fear associated with the disease.

The uninfected family members watched as their family deteriorated, and the uninfected children often had to care for themselves and their sick family members. The children were continuously surrounded by suffering and death while the stigma loomed over the entire family. Family members who were infected and those who were not were all alienated from society. They were all hiding in their homes, ill, isolated and living in fear of the consequences of their disease being revealed. They lived with the constant fear of the persecution they and their families might suffer if somebody found out they had this horrific disease. Shame consumed their lives even if they had done nothing consciously to contract the disease. The nature of the disease prevented them from obtaining the kind of help and sympathy most people suffering from a terminal illness are afforded. Life for them was a nightmare beyond anything which could be imagined.

Infected families had a wide variety of needs which could not be met by the existing male-oriented services. The resources the gay community had formed didn't accommodate a family's needs. The free housing which was available for people with HIV/AIDS consisted of a single room, much like a boarding house, and inappropriate for families with children. The volunteer programs who aided sick males at home was primarily provided by gay men, most who had no skill or desire to assist families and their children. The male-oriented support groups focused on issues which were relevant to gay men only. In the beginning, even case management counselors who were working with people with HIV/AIDS were primarily gay men. Although they were willing to help families, they were at a loss for resources for them.

No matter what the financial health of the family was before the disease struck, most families became destitute and unable to adequately provide for the basic needs of the family. Medical expenses increased as their illness became too severe for them to work. Those who were well enough to work eventually lost their jobs when employers found out they were infected or someone in their family was infected. Periodic bouts of illness prevented them from going to their jobs, and the inconsistency of their attendance due to illness resulted in the loss of their job. Sometimes even the well parents could not provide consistent work performance because they had to take care of another infected family member or their children when the infected parent couldn't. Most were unable to afford childcare. Even if they could, this was not an option because infected children were not allowed to attend child care or public school because of the stigma and fear which existed. Uninfected children of infected parents were also ostracized from usual child activities. Illness overwhelmed these families much of the time. When parents were hospitalized, often no one was willing to take care of their children. Rarely was there extended family willing to help out. Many were alienated from their families because their families blamed them for the life choices they made which resulted in contracting the disease.

The infected who contracted the disease from their drug addiction had additional complex problems. Addicted parents with AIDS were unable to adequately care for their children, particularly their infected children who required intensive medical care. Newborns, born to an infected drug-addicted mother often suffered withdrawal symptoms in addition to being HIV positive. These babies had to be weaned from the effects of the drugs in their system, and often the drug addicted parent was incapable of providing the appropriate care they required. Support without judgment of the parents was imperative in intervening to keep the children safe and cared for. These parents were often on the verge of losing custody of their children, and without intensive intervention they would have been split apart during the short time they had left together.

The complexities of the various needs were endless, and many were unanticipated. Some of the issues these families were dealing with, were unrelated to having a life-threatening disease but were compounded because of the illness. Time intensive support which dealt with their multiple issues was imperative to make sure their children were protected and being cared for.

Fathers whose wives succumbed to the disease and who had not been previously the primary caretaker of their sick or well children needed support with skills for daily living. Adding to the dilemma of caring for their family, these fathers were often infected themselves, creating a multitude of problems impacting their ability to be an adequate caretaker.

The newly diagnosed families had nowhere to turn. After leaving the testing centers, they were left in a state of confusion without any resources to turn to for guidance. They were all shocked and dazed and had no idea what their life was going to be like from that point on. They had just been given a death sentence and didn't have any idea about how to cope with life from that point on. They knew little about the ramifications of the disease. They left the testing centers alone, scared and had the added anxiety of not knowing who else in their family might be infected.

In some instances, the cruel disease drove mothers to abandon their newborns in the hospital because they were unwilling or incapable of taking care of their offspring while they were contending with their own illness. The intense care required, limited life expectancy of the child, health problems of the parents, the tremendous cost of health care and the prejudice of society resulted in at least one-third of infants born testing positive to the virus to be abandoned. Raising and caring for children when one is well can be a difficult task. When weakened by the debilitating impact of AIDS, the obligations of parenthood can become overwhelming. No matter how great the commitment or noble the intent, parents struggling to stay alive may neglect or abandon their children. The only existing alternative for these abandoned infants was to live out their lives in hospitals. These infected orphaned children especially needed a loving environment as they were enduring the ravages of the disease. Rabbi Liza stated, "Children are voiceless - they cannot make demands on their own behalf. For that reason, their needs are even more compelling."

The variety of needs the infected children had were extensive. Foster parents were not an option for infected children because of the fear of transmission and their complex medical needs. Five hundred foster care families, in the Dallas area, were asked if they would consider caring for a child with AIDS. Each one declined. The infected children who had underlying medical conditions, who were entitled to community assistance, were denied services because of their HIV status. Infected children from homeless families were not allowed in shelters. Communities were perplexed about what to do with the orphaned children who were abandoned in hospitals, and nobody had a solution.

Families with children and orphaned children desperately needed a support system to help them live through this devastating disease, and there were none which existed. In the United States, no disease has impacted so many family members at one time in this unique and encompassing way.

5

FORGING FORWARD

Lydia and I started to help the women from the support group by assisting them in the care of their children when the parents were either too ill to care for them or their parent was hospitalized. I would take these children home to my house, and when Lydia was well enough, she would also care for them. There were very few alternatives for these women when they couldn't care for their children.

Maury would sometimes arrive home from work to a house full of toddlers and infants who weren't there when he left for work in the morning. Without hesitation he would roll up his sleeves and go from attorney to caretaker, rocking babies, changing diapers, and feeding children. Tasks which we had not done for many years considering our children were already teenagers. Our teenagers, Kim and Josh, were always willing to pitch in when I arrived home and I had arms full of kids who needed attention.

I was still working full time at Temple Emanu-El, and when the kids of infected parents had no alternative care during the day, I would take them to work with me. I tried to keep a low profile about what I was doing and most people who knew supported my mission and looked the other way when I arrived with children. I would take the children to my office, close the door, and care for them while I managed my other responsibilities. Some people at the synagogue were uncomfortable with me bringing infected children to my office, but the Rabbis ran defense, and theirs was the ultimate word. It was always clear to me, using proper precautions, interactions with these children and mothers was not a risk to me, my family, or bystanders. Many disagreed. We often received skepticism from friends and relatives about the cause we had taken on. Intelligent but uninformed people often accused us of putting other people's lives in jeopardy.

Lydia and I never said out loud to each other that we were going to take care of all the kids who came our way who were affected by AIDS. The mission evolved in both our hearts and propelled us forward. We were two people from very different worlds who came together with a joint mission and pledged to follow our heart's path together. We both had different reasons for embarking on this journey. Lydia was living through the horrors of the disease, and I had an innate, deeply rooted compulsion to help the needy. Our common goal was one of compassion to help children and their families who were the forgotten souls of the AIDS crisis.

As the number of children needing intermittent care increased, I realized I needed to come up with a plan to care for these children and the predicted additional children who were to come. At first, I thought the model I used for the hospital visitation program at Temple Emanu-El might work. I would train volunteers who were comfortable with having contact with people who had AIDS and assign them to go to the homes of these families to help them with their needs. The plan had its flaws.

Soon it became apparent many of these families' home lives were troubled resulting in volunteers being uncomfortable in going to their homes. Additionally, some of the families lived in poverty-stricken environments in dangerous areas of town, which was also not conducive to attracting willing volunteers. Drug use by one or both parents (sometimes the conduit for contracting the disease) presented another deterrent for volunteers. The overall home life for some of the infected families was complex. These environments created a less than desirable assignment for volunteers which often deterred even the most compassionate volunteer. For the most part, volunteers were from very different backgrounds than the families they were trying to help. I also had safety concerns for the volunteers who I was sending into these homes because I feared I could potentially be putting them at risk for reasons other than HIV/AIDS. My first plan was not the solution I had hoped it would be. It also did not resolve the problem of caring for a child when a parent was hospitalized or suddenly orphaned. I finally concluded the plan I had created was inadequate and too risky for all who were involved.

Although the plan I was trying to implement turned out to be flawed, my heart was in the right place, and I was determined to figure out what would work. I didn't dwell on the flaws of the initial plan. I kept moving forward, thought by thought, figuring out what would work. Not for one minute did I doubt there was a solution which would encompass all the variables. The great thing about mistakes is they give you information and teach you about what works and what doesn't. Even though the initial plan did not work out perfectly, the families received assistance while I was figuring out a better idea. I paid attention to all the experiences, all the successes, and failures. I listened to the families and the volunteers and considered the information to formulate the next plan. As I went through the process, I learned more about the reality of what these people were dealing with and the flaws in the existing program. I had a ferocious determination and a lot of faith which forced out the momentary doubts that a solution might not be possible. My mission started with a dream to make life better for people who were drowning with no life jackets in sight, and my commitment to rescue them never wavered.

The complexities of each family's issues were endless. Besides the obvious problems which these families were dealing with because of their illness, there were situations which were unique to each family making the solution very complicated.

Another need which I had to consider in the plan was the dilemma of the children with HIV who were abandoned at birth because they tested positive to the virus. These abandoned infants had only one alternative which was to live out their lives in hospitals. Although the prognosis for some of these children was bleak because they were not expected to live very long, it was imperative to me that they be included in the plan I was formulating. These infants deserved to be in a loving environment, not in a hospital.

Coming up with a solution which would encompass each affected individuals' circumstances was like putting a jigsaw puzzle together while wearing a blindfold.

I needed to develop a unique system of assistance for children and families with HIV/AIDS which took into consideration all the possible variables. No family or child service existed which would accommodate all the aspects of this complex problem. Any program which was going to be effective needed to offer a broad range of services under one roof and be able to adapt to the changing needs in the different stages of the disease. Orphaned children with the disease, and infected children in families, needed the expertise of a facility which could provide medical support in a homelike atmosphere and would be available to them on an ongoing and emergency basis.

The entire family needed support services and case management to cope with their day to day problems. The lives of these families were in constant turmoil and disruption. Efforts to keep the family intact, whenever possible during the illness, was essential. Facilitating the return of children to the parents, when they were well enough to care for them, was a top priority.

While I was working on figuring out how I was going to accomplish this comprehensive plan, I was continuously raising money and donations of goods to meet the needs of the families who we were already helping. They needed financial help for daily essentials. Some needed infant supplies such as immense amounts of diapers to cope with the constant diarrhea of infected children. Keeping infected children dry was essential in preventing potential infections which could become life-threatening. Necessary infant care items and child essentials such as cribs, car seats and clothing were in endless demand. Experts suspected breast milk could carry the virus from mother to child, therefore, it was important that infected mothers did not breastfeed newborns. Infected mothers needed vast amounts of formula to feed their newborns. Acquiring donations was relatively easy. Few could turn away from the plight of families with AIDS, and people were willing to give me whatever I needed for them. Previously, I had never solicited donations of this magnitude from people, but my passion to help propelled me to ask for what I needed without hesitation. I was amazed how assertive I could be when I needed something for these families.

Through trial and error, it became apparent that sending volunteers into people's homes was an imperfect solution for the multitude of problems which these families and children faced. After much thought, I came up with the exact opposite approach. In my mind's eye, I could picture a refuge where children could stay, and families could receive support services. It needed to be a flexible system of care which met the ever-changing needs during the various stages of their disease.

The children needed childcare in a place with a loving, home-like atmosphere when they had to be separated from their parents. Keeping parents and children together as much as possible was an important aspect in providing quality of life for these families who did not have much time left together. It was imperative to provide a consistent environment which was familiar to these children whose home life was completely disrupted. Parents needed a familiar place where they could be confident their children would get out of hospital attentive medical care. I envisioned a home which would be available 24/7 which provided medically managed childcare where children could come and go as needed.

There also was a critical need for the home to be a permanent residence for infected children who no longer had parents. A place which would provide a medically managed, permanent home for infected children whose parents had died or for one reason or another were unable to care for them.

It would take comprehensively meeting every one of these needs to adequately make a difference in the lives of this underserved segment of the AIDS population.

For the plan to be successful, the ideal facility would need to provide the entire family with a continuum of care, coordinating health care, case management, care for their infected and well children and permanent care for children who no longer had parents.

I pondered the details of the problem for many hours and days. It took over almost my every thought. It was critical to the lives of these children and families that I come up with a way to help in this untenable situation. I couldn't do anything about the underlying cause of their tragic situation, but I was determined to improve their quality of life until it ended.

No one in the Dallas/Fort Worth area or around the country was focusing on a comprehensive plan to encompass the full spectrum of assistance infected children and families needed. It was solely up to Lydia and me to make it happen. I constantly vacillated between thinking this plan was so complicated that it wasn't possible to encompass all the aspects in one facility and other times I was utterly confident that I could create a solution. For brief moments I would become insecure and think about my lack of experience or education in all the elements needed to accomplish what I was trying to do. When those thoughts entered my mind, I knew I had to suppress them, or all would be lost. During those times I had to force myself to focus on the end result and plow forward with determination.

The number of infected women and children was rapidly increasing as I tried to figure out how to go forward. It became more and more imperative to act as quickly as possible. In creating my paintings, before the brush touches the canvas, I see the end result in my mind's eye. I consider every brush stroke and how it will affect the finished painting. I consider every detail, focusing on how it will fit into the big picture. The attention to every detail is critical to be successful. My approach to figuring out how an assistance program of this magnitude was a similar process. I pictured the solution and focused on every detail which needed to be included to make the big picture work. I envisioned what an ideal result would look like to meet all the needs of these children and their families before I proceeded to make the first stroke.

Lydia and I began to look for model programs around the country which were providing assistance to families and children. We soon found out there were none. The only models which seemed to exist were not all-encompassing. The programs which were trying to help infected children and families only addressed limited aspects of their needs. Most infected abandoned children lived in hospitals, and the only foster facility for infected children we could locate was St. Clare's in New Jersey. A few hospitals around the country had outpatient services and limited assistance for families. None of the programs encompassed a comprehensive continuum of care for all the aspects of this complex problem.

As the details of what was needed began to become clear in my mind, I started to construct a program that I thought would work. Each element had a solution but integrating it all into the final picture was the challenge. Clearly, I had no prior knowledge of what it would take to create a comprehensive solution which met all the various needs, but I was unrelenting. Fortunately, being inexperienced, I had no preconceived limitations or any knowledge of any future obstacles which would make me think I couldn't accomplish the impossible. Obstacles just became challenges to overcome. Together with Lydia's medical expertise and her first-hand experience living with the disease, we began brainstorming endlessly.

Lydia found out the Second Annual Pediatric AIDS Conference was about to be held in New York in April of 1988. We decided we would attend so we could avail ourselves of any information which existed. We also wanted to observe St. Clare's foster home which was not too far away from the conference. As we gained knowledge of the needs and the lack of solutions, the picture of what we needed to do started to become more evident.

Lydia was personally and medically knowledgeable about families' needs, and I had the vision and confidence to make our plan happen. We made a good team, but she was always fearful her involvement would again expose her family to prejudice and persecution. At her request, I committed to keeping her and her family's situation in the shadows, safe from public scrutiny. We were both well aware of the ramifications for her and her family which could be devastating, and I was fastidious about keeping her secret.

Our plan of how we were going to help HIV/AIDS families began to take shape. I still didn't know all the details of how I was going to make it work, but each step brought us closer to the answers. Fortunately, I never really focused on the enormity of it all or I might have been paralyzed and unable to move forward. I had no insight into all the challenges yet to come. I just kept putting one foot in front of the other, overcoming one problem at a time to achieve the desired result and kept charging forward.

The first step to start taking our objective from the planning stages to implementation was to gather people who had walked similar paths. Rabbi Liza assembled a group of women from the synagogue to mentor me. This group of women, older than me and very accomplished, were respected social action leaders in the community. They were founders and supporters of many respected community services in Dallas. As volunteers, these women were all devoted to making this world a better place. Beverly Tobian, a recipient of the Maura Award for Women

Helping Women, was the founder of the Women's Council of the Health and Human Services Coalition. She worked with The Family Place to stop family violence, New Life Prostitution Division Initiative, and the Older Women's League — just a few of her endeavors to help people in need. Sylvia Benenson had a deep and abiding commitment to a variety of social concerns. She was a board member of the Volunteer Center and founding member of the Family Outreach Center. Syl served on the Social Services Committee of the Martin Luther King Community Center, Safeguards for Seniors Project, the board of North Texas Refugee Interagency, and the Vietnamese Community of Greater Dallas Coalition for Public Health. Doris Budner was co-founder and President of the Dallas Coalition for The Homeless. She was the co-founder of the Vogel Alcove Childcare Center for The Homeless, which provided daycare for homeless children. Doris served in a leadership role on more than 30 community boards including United Way, Success by Six, Child and Family Guidance Center, Family Gateway, and North Texas Food Bank. Hortense Sanger volunteered, chaired, and founded many charitable causes in Dallas, including Visiting Nurse Association, Hope Cottage, East Dallas Health Coalition, Goals for Dallas, The Dallas Alliance, Rhoads Terrace School, and the Crossroads Center, to name just a few.

These influential women were lifelong movers and shakers in the Dallas community long before women were asserting their power. Each one volunteered their time, and I mean a lot of time, to care for the helpless, homeless, and sick. They knew everyone with power in the city, and everyone knew not to stand in the way of these powerful women. These inspiring women gave me the gift of their experience and the gumption to push on.

Dallas is a large city in geographical size and population but has the overall feel of a small town. Despite its size, Dallas is unique in the fact that community leaders are readily accessible. Being able to access the political leaders in the city was valuable and somewhat easier than in most large metropolitan areas. These leaders were willing to help us because the city had a crisis on its hands and no resources to provide services for the exploding population of people with AIDS. They needed our help, and we needed theirs. Maury and I also had a wide range of social and business acquaintances in diverse areas of expertise, which helped immensely.

We assembled a Board of Directors consisting of some of the women mentioned above, and recruited doctors and lawyers, rabbis and ministers, child care experts, and several influential members of the community. As always, Maury was by my side every step of the way. He became the founding Chairman of the Board for the organization. After much contemplation, we named our non-profit organization the "Care Coalition." Maury did all the legal work for us to be incorporated and obtain a non-profit status. We were finally off and running, and I truly mean running!

Not too long after, we discovered the name "Care Coalition" was already in use, but the entity had not legally registered the name. We decided, even though we could use the name legally, it would have caused confusion in the non-profit world. We decided to rename the organization. On March 22, 1988, the Articles of Incorporation were amended, and the name Open Arms, Inc. was adopted. We included a tagline in the logo which read "Open arms, open hearts, and open minds." Our mission statement was established as "A medically managed home, for children 0 to 11 years of age who were affected by AIDS. Providing day care, respite care, permanent residential care, and supportive services for the entire family at no cost."

With Rabbi Liza's fervent support and guidance from the beginning we forged forward. Listening to her words, infused with wisdom and compassion, continuously instilled confidence in me to take the next step in my journey. She helped me climb the ladder of challenges with courage. Her words gave me the confidence to be a leader.

My theory is "Good things come to those who *don't* wait!" Dream it, do the research, learn everything you can about the subject, and go forth without hesitation. And that's precisely what we did.

6

THE BIRTH OF A HAVEN

After Lydia and I returned from the Pediatric AIDS Conference, we felt we had gathered all the information about existing programs for children with AIDS that was available, which was not very much. People who were involved in pediatric HIV/AIDS services were just in the early stages of trying to serve this population, so we were on our own to execute a continuum of care which would encompass the broad range of problems this population was dealing with.

Next step was to figure out how we were going to finance this ambitious idea. My first thought was to contact the executive director of the Design Industries Foundation Fighting AIDS (DIFFA). Maury and I had a close relationship with the Executive Director, Steve Burrus, and I felt he would be sympathetic about what we were trying to do. As dedicated volunteers for the organization, Maury and I helped raise money for research and services, participating in a movement to help do what the government was not doing. I explained to Steve, I had recently become aware that there were families and children who were living in the shadows of the gay men's crisis and nobody was providing any services to meet their unique needs. Even though he was immersed in the AIDS dilemma, he was surprised to hear about the plight of these families who were also enduring immense suffering. I explained my plan and what needed to be done to help the families who desperately needed support services and a safety net for the orphaned children who were affected. As he sat there stunned by this enlightening revelation, I told him about my plans to rent a house where I could take care of the children. I then dropped the bomb that I needed some funding from DIFFA to make it all happen. I told him, I felt sure I could get everything else I needed donated, including volunteers to take care of the children. After the look of shock left his face, he agreed to give me $5,000. It was not a lot of money for what I was attempting to do, but I knew it would enable me to at least rent a house and pay utilities for three months. When we were up and running Steve confessed to me that he had his doubts about whether I was going to be able to accomplish this crazy idea. At the time, I wasn't sure I could pull it off either. I was grateful for Steve's empathy, and his confidence in me which compelled him to take a leap of faith.

The money available for services and research was very scarce. The gay community was fighting for every dollar, and many felt threatened by Lydia and me bringing children into the fight for dollars. They maintained there were far fewer children infected with the virus opposed to the number of gay men who needed help and there wasn't enough money to go around as it was. Additionally, they were concerned children were a more sympathetic cause and therefore, it would be easier for us to tap the limited funds which were available. To some degree it was true.

As in many cities across the country, Dallas leaders found themselves in the midst of a crisis without financial resources allocated to fund the needed services. Dallas needed to mobilize resources as quickly as possible, and the city leaders needed help from the community to do it. They needed citizens to create and implement services, and we needed the city's support and cooperation in finding funding sources.

In an attempt to create services to support the infected, the Dallas County Planning Commission formed a task force to focus on the problems and develop partnerships with community organizations who were in the trenches helping people with HIV/AIDS. Their main focus was on the gay community because the plight of women and children with AIDS was not considered to be a major problem because there was significantly fewer cases then the men who were infected. I had to aggressively force my way onto the task force to become the sole representative of women and children. As one of the few people involved in their plight, I had to be their voice and demand they be considered in the solution to the problem. The commission's report "AIDS, A Community Response," highlighted the statistics and services needed to address the issue. The report was approximately 380 pages long, and when it was completed only 2 pages addressed the needs of children and their families with HIVAIDS. Once again, reaffirming the notion to many that women and children were not a significant problem in the overall dilemma.

Confronting the fact that Lydia and I were on our own to meet the needs of women and children, we set out on our journey to establish the refuge we envisioned. With $5,000 from DIFFA and a lot of hope, we took the first steps to find a house and raise additional funds. Neither Lydia nor I had any experience in grant writing. We plunged into the process and figured out how to write grants to ensure we could finance our endeavor. Also, I asked everybody I knew for donations. We were diligent in our search for funds because we were keenly aware that the $5,000 we had from DIFFA, was not going to last very long. It wasn't too long before we realized we were handicapped in our fundraising efforts because most major funders wanted demonstrated operating history and we had none.

Additionally, we could not verify how many children and families needed help because the statistics for families and children who were actually infected, was an unknown number, but we didn't let that stop us, we just forged ahead. Estimates showed Texas had the fifth largest number of pediatric AIDS cases in the United States. The state health department was predicting 282 children would be born HIV positive in 1988. The disparity between predicted pediatric AIDS cases and reported cases was problematic in every city creating a problem in obtaining funding.

Lydia and I applied to every pocket of money we could think of. I asked every source of funding I knew to donate to the cause. After DIFFA'S $5,000, Temple Emanu-El and the Women's Foundation of Dallas were the next to grant us funds. We became grant-writing machines. We soon discovered it was a numbers game. Submit as many grants as humanly possible, and inevitably some would be approved. We put all our energy into finding applicable grants. We feverishly researched every organization who provided funding for anything related or somewhat related to what we were trying to accomplish. We applied to funders who supported AIDS, childcare, homeless children, health care, foster homes, religious organizations (between us we had influence with two denominations) and any other sources which were even slightly related. Also, I had contacts in the community who were typically generous donors, and I contacted every one of them to donate funds or to provide items which we needed for maintaining the refuge.

Another source of funding which initially was not available to us was from the elite in Dallas. The affluent in the Dallas community are champions of charity work. They have an extraordinary ability to put on elaborate fundraisers which financially supports many of the community's services. Their support was eventually an invaluable asset for our fundraising efforts, but it took some time to gain acceptance into the "favored charity circuit." For many of these organizations, raising funds to support children with AIDS became a way of helping out during the AIDS crisis without having to make any moral judgments related to the gay lifestyle.

Still, the ongoing difficulty of raising funds remained the inability to verify the number of children who needed help. Funders wanted us to quantify how many children there were with HIV/AIDS needing our help, and we had no earthly idea, and neither did anybody else. The numbers of infected children remained a common request from funders because they logically wanted to use their available dollars to assist organizations who were helping the most significant number of people in need. Initially, we had first-hand knowledge of about a dozen or so children who we were already assisting, and we had heard about others who had not come forth, and who would inevitably need our help. We were sure there were more, but they were living in seclusion because of the risk of revealing that they had the disease. Also, there were not any services available to them, therefore there was not any reason for them to take that risk. Having few verifiable numbers of infected children was a hindrance in our quest for the large amount of money we needed to sustain the project. All we could do was to state the statistic of the predicted numbers. Statistically, the rapid rate of new infections in women indicated there would soon be many more children and entire families needing help. Estimates from all the professionals were different, but that was not the answer some funders wanted to hear.

In 1988 the Dallas County Health Department estimated they expected 40 to 45 babies to be born to infected mothers in Dallas County that year.

There were a lot of factors involved in not being able to accurately assess the number of the infected children. Private doctors often did not report the infected to the health department because they wanted to protect the family's anonymity. Additionally, there was a population of infected mothers and their children, who for some time, did not know they were infected; therefore, they had not yet come forth. Reported statistics only reflected the children with full blown AIDS and did not include children who were HIV positive. Also, infected families were migrating to Dallas from surrounding counties to seek health care because their local health care providers were not knowledgeable about the treatment of the disease. There was no way to determine how many of these families would be needing help. In addition to all the variables preventing us from coming up with accurate numbers of the infected, we couldn't determine the number of uninfected family members who we were also going to be providing services to. Each time we had to answer the numbers question, it felt like we were dancing on the head of a pin, trying to avoid providing verifiable numbers of women and children who we were going to serve.

As we searched for funds, we often had to meet with funders to plead our case about the unprovable unmet needs of the people we were trying to help. Throughout the process, Lydia was adamant about not letting the people we met with know she and her family were amongst the infected. It was somewhat uncomfortable as the funders talked about "those families" without using the sensitivity they would have used if they had known Lydia was infected.

As we worked on getting funding, the number of children who we were helping was increasing, and we had no time to wait for all the money we needed to operate before we took further action. Lydia was pretty skeptical about whether we could pull it off, but she was willing to follow my lead.

With the $5,000 in hand we began our search for a property. The criteria for the ideal property was extensive and our funds were extremely limited and prospects for additional funding was tenuous at best.

Up to this point, everything was in the planning stage. Suddenly, it felt like we were now about to make the first big commitment which would take this monumental undertaking from planning to actually existing.

When we embarked on the search for a physical place to implement our plan, I pictured a place which looked like a warm, inviting home. I didn't want it to stand out in the neighborhood. I wanted it to look like all the other houses on the street, not like an orphanage or institution or some commercial endeavor. People were fearful of being around anyone with the disease, so we had to find a property which was inconspicuous, and in an area where people were less likely to object to our presence. We concluded the Oaklawn area of Dallas seemed to fit the bill. Oaklawn is primarily a gay residential and entertainment hub mixed in with middle-income homes which were mostly owned by Hispanic families. We assumed our presence would be less controversial there because the people who were living in the area were already open to living in a gay community with the unknowns about HIV/AIDS. We could not be sure our assumptions were correct, so it was essential no matter where we ended up, we needed to maintain a very low profile until we could reassure the neighbors that our presence was not a risk to them.

An additional advantage to finding a suitable house in the Oak Lawn area was the majority of existing AIDS service providers for the gay community were located there and they had some services which would be useful to our families.

We had to find a property which maximized the bedroom space. Department of Human Services (DHS) required 40 square feet of bedroom space per child, therefore the space in the bedrooms dictated how many children we could accommodate. We were constrained by our limited funds and had to make sure the property we picked had large bedrooms or other rooms we could designate as bedrooms.

We needed to be centrally located and near public transportation, so families could easily access our services.

Another important consideration was to be near Children's Medical Center (CMC) and Parkland Hospital where the majority of medical care was being provided to the infected.

The surrounding area needed to be conducive for volunteers to be comfortable coming to so that we would have enough help taking care of the children. Volunteers were of primary importance to stretching our limited funds.

Our quest for an appropriate property led us to an intense real estate hunt. We looked at every available property which fit our parameters in the Oak Lawn and surrounding areas. We considered empty churches, abandoned houses, a convent which was no longer in use. We looked at rentals and lease for purchase properties and any other building which had at least some potential. If the square footage met our needs, I felt confident I could adapt the remainder of the property to work for us but finding a place which met all the essential criteria with our financial constraints made our search feel hopeless at times.

The first property we seriously considered was four attached condominiums which were for sale. The initial plan was to rent a place for a few months until we could accumulate more money, so we proposed a rent to buy option to the owner. It was in the targeted neighborhood, and we considered breaking through each one of the units to make one contiguous unit. We thought it might work, but we ran into an obstacle. There was an element in the gay community who was threatened by our existence and they attempted to sabotage the deal we were trying to make. The man who owned the property had AIDS and was suffering from dementia which was common to people in the advance stages of the disease. Our adversaries took advantage of the owner's dementia and convinced him we were offering him a bad deal and after negotiations, we lost the property. Again, we encountered the resentment from particular factions in the gay community towards us. Mainly it was about the limited dollars available for AIDS services and the fear we would be impacting their resources.

We were discouraged momentarily, but it wasn't long before we were back out pounding the pavement to find a place that would meet our criteria. The second property we considered seemed to have potential. Again, this property was listed for sale and not for rent. It was a 1940s brown, weathered, two-story English Tudor style house. English Tudor sounds lavish, but it wasn't even close to lavish. The house had space heaters and no air conditioning and needed a lot of TLC. Towards the back of the property there was an additional small building on the property which was referred to as the "Quarters." The small building was a tiny one-room structure with a bathroom. As we toured the house, I was envisioning how each area could be converted to serve our needs best. The quarters, as small as they were, seemed like it might work for office space.

The main house was approximately 2200 sq. ft. Upon entering the front door, there was a large living room which had wood floors and a long bank of cabinets. I pictured the living room would be a perfect playroom and the cabinets would work for storage of toys. To the left of the living room was a dining room which led to a large bright kitchen with all the essential appliances. The living room and the kitchen led to a large center hall with a bathroom off of it. I imagined turning the hall into a diaper changing station. The wide stairs in the hall led to a second story with two large bedrooms and one small one. The large bathroom on the second floor had all the essentials including a large claw foot tub which was perfect for bathing several children at one time. The entire house had oversized windows which drew in the sunlight creating a cheerful atmosphere.

The kitchen had glass sliding doors which provided an alternate entrance into the house from the rear of the building. The glass doors led to a small deck in the backyard. The backyard, between the house and the small building was large enough to put in a sizeable playground for the children.

Adjacent to the property was a large empty corner lot which had two small broken-down houses on it. We were told there had been a church on the land, which burned down, leaving the two little houses standing. The realtor told us vagrants and drug dealers were occupying the houses. Not the most comforting aspect of the property. As we toured, I secretly fantasized the empty lot would be perfect for us to expand our capacity. At the time, I didn't realize how quickly the need for more space would become imperative.

The home was located at 2713 Knight Street in the Oaklawn area of Dallas. Geographically it was perfect. The house was nestled in at the end of a block of small houses. It was a cozy neighborhood with tree-lined streets. The neighborhood had a combination of apartments and condos interspersed with small houses. On one side of the house was a family with lots of children and the empty lot was on the other side. At least on one side, we didn't have to be concerned about the neighbors having a problem with our presence. I was hoping we could get permission to use the empty lot for parking, so parents and guests could enter through the back of the house limiting activity on the street side in front of the house. Also, confidentiality was a continuous concern for the infected parents, so inconspicuously entering from the rear of the house, could prove to be a big advantage. The rear entrance would also help us to maintain a low profile in the neighborhood. We were sensitive to the fact that most communities would not have been comfortable with having a home for children with AIDS located where they were living. We had enough to deal with without having a problem with the neighbors.

The property seemed almost perfect except for the fact the house was for sale, and we only had enough money to rent a property and pay utilities for a few months. Somehow, I convinced the owner to temporarily rent it to us. I assured him, as soon as I received the funds we had applied for, I would buy it from him. The owner, Ron Hamby, was a kind man and sympathetic to our cause. He understood the urgency of our need to provide a safety net for the children, and he agreed to lease it to us with the right to purchase it when we could.

Our lease began on July 1, 1988 and we were off and running towards our mission. We immediately began renovating using donated goods and services to adapt it to function for our purpose. Every day a varied army of volunteers would show up including Maury, my kids, my parents, my friends and acquaintances, and sympathetic strangers who worked diligently to make the house ready to care for kids. I called in every contact I knew and some who I didn't personally know: contractors, plumbers, painters, friends who had custom curtains and bedding, and an air conditioning company who gave us central heat and air. I contacted a hardware store and got all the materials donated which we needed for the renovations. I contacted a security company and asked them to give us a security system and the ongoing monitoring. Rarely did anyone turn me down. Everyone I knew gave me furniture, toys, household goods, baby food, tons of diapers, formula and I could go on and on but let it suffice to say I got every last item I needed donated.

We were finally at the point where we had a house which was still a work in progress, and we had some money in the bank, but there was still a lot to do before we were up and running. When we returned from the Pediatric AIDS Conference, armed with information, our plan began to solidify. It was only about three months from the time when we began to implement the plan until we had a facility, but it felt like a lifetime. Sometimes it felt like we were getting closer to the opening, but around each corner, there was another monumental obstacle to overcome.

The entire time we were working on the house, I kept thinking about the number of families who we were already helping, and the predictions of the inevitable number of people who would need our help in the not too distant future. We had to start somewhere which made financial sense until we were able to raise more money. This place, although it was limited in space for what we would ultimately need, seemed like a good start. I knew expansion was inevitable and seeing an empty property next door had my imagination on overdrive even though I did not know anything about its availability at the time.

I was continuously concerned about the neighbors finding out about what we were doing in the little house on Knight Street because I feared all our progress could have been lost if they objected to our presence. Every time I heard about an incident of persecution of people with AIDS, it sent a shiver up my spine. Families with AIDS were being driven out of their neighborhoods all too often. I knew no matter what neighborhood we settled in, we were going to have the same concern. I suppressed the fear, so it would not distract me from all the other issues which I needed to focus on. I tried not to think about the ramifications of a neighborhood uprising.

While we were working on the renovations of the house, I was taking every opportunity to build a cordial relationship with the neighbors to avert any potential problems. I tried to tone down any blatant activities which would bring attention to the house, but on Halloween night before we opened, that strategy backfired. On that night, the house was alive with volunteers working, so when children came trick or treating, I couldn't avoid answering the door. My concern was when parents found out we were housing children with HIV/AIDS and we had given their children candy, they might have become alarmed. Using an overabundance of caution, I handed out a donation we received of Hot Wheel Cars to the Trick-or-Treaters. Inadvertently, the special treats brought unwanted attention to our house and when word got around there were lines of children at our door.

7

STUMBLING BLOCKS

During the time the renovations were going on, we had raised $41,658 and had $952,165 pending from grants and private funders who had not yet decided whether they would fund us. I stretched every dollar as far as it would go. Funds were only spent on rent, utilities, and contaminated trash removal, and everything else was donated. The $41,658 gave us a slight sense of security considering we started with $5,000, but there still was a long way to go to be able to care for the increasing numbers of children who were emerging from the shadows.

As the renovations were coming to completion, the house was beginning to look like the vision I had intended. With volunteers and donated items, the house was evolving into a place which would accommodate the needs of the infected children and their families.

We left the outside of the house as it was, so it would blend in with the neighborhood avoiding any dissension from a fearful community. The house looked like any other house on the street, but upon entry, after the renovations, the inside was a child's wonderland. Walking through the front door, a burst of primary colors would entice any child or visitor. I decorated the walls throughout the house with green turtles, yellow rabbits, red horses, and blue elephants. The bank of cabinets, across from the front door was painted the same green, yellow, red, and blue overflowing with donated toys for all ages. My objective was to create an atmosphere which would resemble a fantasy land for children. If a visitor somehow unknowingly entered the house and didn't notice the medical equipment, it would appear it was a place where privileged children lived. These kids were facing an existence of severe illness and pain along with being deprived of a traditional loving family and it was imperative to me that they have a glorious home to live out their dying days.

Converting an old house into a child care facility, which would accommodate the children's and staff's needs, was just the beginning of the many challenges to overcome. I designed every aspect to be the ultimate in efficiency. Containment of bodily fluids was of utmost importance. Safety precautions to protect the uninfected was always a major consideration in my design elements. I used the center hall for a changing station but the disposal of diapers which contained bodily fluids was a perplexing dilemma because traditional diaper pails were inadequate in preventing the spread of infection. I resolved the problem by installing trash compactors beside each changing table for diaper disposal. The unique use of trash compactors reduced the risk of contact with bodily fluids for staff and volunteers during the disposal of the many diapers. The ceiling over the changing tables was open to the second story. Carrie Clammer, a graphic artist, designed and built an enormous mobile duplicating the same brightly colored animals which were on the walls. The mobile hung over the changing tables to entertain the children during a not so enjoyable activity.

Stefanie holding an infant in front of Bryan's House.

The kitchen and all the other rooms were designed to have the warmth of a typical home.

My mother who became an interior designer later in her life, tented the ceiling of the large bathroom upstairs to make it look like a circus tent. She commissioned artists to paint brightly colored circus icons on the walls. Each of the bedrooms had brightly colored cribs and small toddler beds with custom bedding and curtains to match. All the decor was accomplished without spending any of our funds. My mother, Maury, Kim and Josh worked tirelessly to make my vision exactly how I wanted it to be. My mother Beverly faithfully indulged my artistic aspirations. She supervised painters and workers with meticulous execution of every detail. Maury and Josh worked on the yard and took it from a muddy mess and made it into a vision of distinction. Not being licensed yet we couldn't "officially" be taking care of children, so while we were working on the house, my daughter Kim would "unofficially" help take care of the children who needed immediate care.

One day, unexpectedly, a group of volunteers arrived and tore down the existing weathered deck at the rear of the house and built a large deck with a handicap ramp.

Donations would arrive steadily, and everyone who was there would stop what they were doing and haul them in. Without hesitation, everyone would pitch in willingly to do anything which needed to be done. My enthusiasm was boundless and contagious, and the house was constantly alive with excitement.

Volunteers came from every walk of life. Dr. Richard Wasserman, a Pediatric Allergy and Immunology doctor, who was on our board, and one of the few doctors in the city caring for children with HIV, was often seen with his son mowing the lawn on his days off. It was heartwarming to see people give of themselves, participating in acts of kindness to improve the quality of life for these children in need. I asked everyone I encountered to help with the mission. Some gave donated time, some gave money, and some gave freely of their goods and services. It amazed me that people didn't run the other way when they saw me coming, because everyone I knew was sure I would be asking for something I needed for the children and almost everyone gave willingly.

The backyard, previously barren, was transformed into a child's amusement park. Hal Karp, a member of the Young Adult Action Committee at Temple Emanu-El, designed the playground for the children. He coordinated with St. Luke's Community United Methodist Church and together they erected a little bit of heaven for the kids. One of the many gratifying occurrences was the unification of many faiths working together for a common cause. This young man raised $8,000 to fund the project and gathered volunteers who all came with their own tools. The playground equipment was thoughtfully tailored to adapt to the unique needs of this population. It was complete with a soft surface on the ground which reduced the chances of injuries which might cause bleeding and could put the uninfected in jeopardy. On the weekend before the playground was to be built, the volunteer's optimism was shattered. In the dark of the night, all the tools which the volunteers had assembled for the project were stolen. It was a disheartening setback for these young, enthusiastic volunteers who were trying to do a good deed. Thanks to the media, all was not lost. An article appeared in the paper on Sunday in the Dallas Morning News about the theft, and during the following week, strangers from various walks of life arrived at our door with donations of replacement tools.

Bryan's House special needs playground.

Next challenge was obtaining all the licensing required to operate the facility. When I started, it was all about helping people whose lives were being devastated. Naively, it never entered my mind, that in doing so, I would be dealing with licensing and regulations beyond my wildest dreams. At each step, there was another part of the puzzle I had to figure out. All the restrictions made my head spin!

The first major obstacle threatened our very existence. The Department of Human Services informed us regulations prohibited doing multiple types of services in one facility. The existing licenses stipulated they were only granted for daycare providers or foster group homes. Offering one kind of care was not going to be adequate to serve this populations needs comprehensively. The limitations were threatening to be disastrous to the overall intention of our solution of being a refuge for children who needed various types of care at different times. It was essential to be flexible and able to provide day care, respite care, and residential care to meet the needs of the children. It was necessary to do daycare for children with HIV who were excluded from traditional childcare centers. Parents needed the availability of respite care 24/7 when they were too ill to care for their children, or the parent had to be hospitalized. Permanent care was also essential for children who no longer had parents. After harrowing negotiations with the state, they conceded, allowing me to apply for a waiver which would allow me to create a unique childcare license for all our anticipated services. Once again, I had to learn about, and find a solution to, an aspect of our goal which I knew nothing about and never anticipated. DHS had the incentive to approve this unique system of childcare because they didn't have an alternative for these children.

DHS was desperate to find placement for the growing number of children in these circumstances. Therefore, they were willing to work with us. They did not have any resources to meet the needs of these families or any experience in providing services to a family who had multiple people with this fatal disease.

After the battle to change the licensing regulations to include various types of care under one roof, we were informed of another unanticipated dilemma. It was mandatory that we have a licensed Child Care Administrator on site to supervise the home. Clearly, we could not afford to hire one. OK, another obstacle. How do I overcome this one? We couldn't afford to hire one, so my only alternative was to become one. Easier said than done! To be eligible to become one, the regulations stated, I needed to submit three professional references attesting to my work experience in childcare. I didn't have any formal experience in childcare. I never did it in any qualifying way. Next, submit evidence of one-year management in a residential child care setting. Nope, didn't have that either. The regulations stated they would waive the experience if I had a master's or doctoral degree relevant to childcare. I went to art school, and they didn't teach administration of a child care facility there! Pass a criminal check. That one was easy.

The last requirement was passing a comprehensive test to qualify for the license. DHS made exceptions for all the other requirements, but I did have to take the test. It was apparent they were desperate for the services which we were going to be providing, and therefore they were willing to bend the rules for lack of experience, but not for the test. I got the materials and studied, and studied, and studied, while I was working on everything else which needed to be done. Low and behold, I passed with the proverbial flying colors and got licensed as a Child Care Administrator. DHS justified making the exceptions on my lack of experience or education in the field by requiring me to be supervised for the first six months by a Licensed Child Care Administrator. Fortunately, I had a friend and colleague from Temple Emanu-El who was a Licensed Child Care Administrator. Nita Mae Tannenbaum, an expert in the child care arena, and a committed supporter of our mission, consented to be my supervisor.

When I embarked on this mission, I was singly focused on trying to help women and children who were in utter agony as the result of a cruel and unrelenting disease. Again naively, I never anticipated all the stumbling blocks that I would have to overcome to accomplish what my heart was propelling me to do. As I conquered each part of the mission, I went on to the next step towards the finish line. I hadn't thought about the fact, which I believed to be the finish line, was just the beginning of the mission. Sometime during the process of acquiring my Child Care Administrator's license I began to realize I was destined to oversee the entire program. Only after becoming the administrator, did the profound realization come to me, I was going to be responsible for the lives of every child who entered the doors of this intended haven.

Just when I thought I was getting close to being done jumping through all the hoops and I could finally start taking care of the kids who were waiting in the wings needing immediate attention, I was confronted with more obstacles to overcome.

The renovations were almost completed, funding was going well, and I was granted my Child Care Administrators license. What more could I need? Well, I found out! To complete the licensing requirements to occupy the house, I had to get a "green tag" from the city which included approval from building inspectors, the Health Department and the Fire Department. Only after all these inspections passed the regulations, and I received a Certificate of Occupancy (CO), could we begin providing childcare. The process of becoming a fully approved, functional facility, felt endless...

At first, I didn't know what a CO was, but like all the other hoops I had to jump through, I soon learned. In the beginning, as far as I knew I had to raise some money, rent a house, and move into it and start caring for children! I found out it wasn't exactly reality. To occupy the home for childcare, we needed a CO. The city inspectors who granted the CO stepped right up to inform me of the numerous violations we had to correct before we could be granted the CO.

Complying with the Health Department was a relatively simple task compared to the other regulations. Because we were going to be doing medical care in a licensed child care facility and also providing meals, there were specific requirements. They gave me written regulations to follow, and I implemented them.

The next alteration I had to make to get the CO was not so easy. The house had quite a few windows which enhanced its charm until we found out they were too low to the ground to be safe for the children. Getting plexiglass donated and replacing all the windows with it was only one of the unexpected alterations we had to make.

We had to make many changes in the interior to comply, but there was one requirement which the fire department had which ended up being a major quagmire. According to my plan, at night we would have one child care worker on the second floor where up to nine children would potentially be sleeping. The Fire Department required an escape plan which would enable a childcare worker to be able to get all the children out of the second floor in case there was a fire. I racked my brain to figure something out. Sounds like a small problem compared to what I had already conquered, but it wasn't. I spent many hours trying figure out a solution. I thought maybe an airline escape ramp would work, or maybe a garbage shoot used by demolition companies. Anything that already existed seemed impractical and probably unobtainable. The evacuation solution had to be resolved immediately and without spending any money. It ended up being the last major obstacle which was holding us up from opening.

From day one, the urgency to open quickly was ever present. Kids were falling through the cracks of the epidemic, and I believed it was up to me to save them. I just kept going from one hurdle to the next. Thankfully, I didn't know there was always going to be another hurdle ahead to overcome. My perception was

I was running as fast as I could, but it was never fast enough. In reality, everything was happening at lightning speed. It just never felt fast enough.

To resolve the escape plan, I designed a wood ramp which went from a large second story window to the ground. At the top of the ramp, was a large wooden box, big enough to fit all the children and the childcare attendant inside. I devised a pulley system, attached to the box and the ramp, which would enable the child care worker to lower the box to the ground. The wood and the hardware were donated, and volunteers built it in one weekend. Great idea, but after it was completed, I couldn't get the Fire Department to approve it because it was flammable. Back to the hypothetical drawing board! I researched options and fortunately found a company who had paint which could be applied to the wood which would make it flameproof. I contacted the company and got it donated in exchange for publicity for their product.

On the first trial run, we loaded the child care worker into the box with several stuffed animals to simulate the children. It worked well until it got to the bottom when it flipped over and dumped the child care worker and the zoo of stuffed animals onto the ground. A few more tries and adjustments and it solved the dilemma, and the Fire Department approved it.

Added to the challenges of overcoming all the obstacles, I not only had to metaphorically reinvent the wheel, but I had to get the wheel donated.

The number of new learning experiences, to comply with all the rules and regulations, challenged me daily during the process of actually seeing the vision become a reality. Overcoming the constant flow of problems, dilemmas and the doubts of others constantly swirled around me like a tornado.

We were in the final phase of completing all the requirements for all the entities when I received an urgent call about a child needing an emergency placement. The call came from the AIDS Resource Center (ARC). They were reaching out to me in desperation because they had a situation they were not accustomed to dealing with and needed help. ARC was an organization who provided a multitude of assistance programs to gay men with AIDS. They were also the agency which had been a vocal adversary of our mission. They wanted to know if we could take care of an uninfected 8-year-old boy. He needed immediate care. Volunteers at ARC discovered this boy was the sole caretaker of a man who was in his last stages of the disease. They were transporting the man to the hospital and didn't' know what to do with the boy.

We were still waiting for our license to be approved, and I was concerned about doing anything which would jeopardize getting our final approval. I contacted our licensing agent to see if I could make an exception and care for the boy. Understanding our dilemma, she figured out a way around the regulations. She had not issued the license yet, therefore we could still be considered a private home and we could care for the boy.

That was only part of the problem enabling us to care for the boy. At that point, no one was at the house at night, and I had to figure out who was going to stay with him. I was overwhelmed with what I needed to do to get our doors open, and Lydia was not up to taking on the responsibility, so I needed to find someone willing to stay at night.

My parents, Beverly and Al Sidd, had just retired, and I asked them if they would stay with the boy. Without hesitation, they moved in and became the House Parents. They remained there until we were up and running and able to hire staff. We were off and running before we even opened our doors. It was only the beginning of an avalanche of children who were affected by the disease and who were urgently needing our care.

It was somewhat ironic that our first resident came from ARC because initially they were vehemently opposed to our existence. They were also the organization who interfered with us trying to buy the four condo units. In all fairness, they were trying to care for so many men compared to the number of women and children who we were trying to help. Every organization was scrambling for the limited funds which were available for AIDS services, and it created animosity between agencies. Also, infected women and children were considered, by the public at large, to be the innocent victims in the crisis, causing ill will from some in the gay community who maintained that everyone with the disease was an innocent victim.

The dad of the young boy died, leaving us with the child who had no idea who his relatives were. Maury embarked on a search for relatives who would qualify to accept guardianship of him. As the search evolved, Maury ascertained the man who the boy was caring for was not his biological father and did not have legal custody of him. Through Maury's research, he discovered, when the child was born, the man happened to be in the hospital at the same time the boy's mother was giving birth. The man apparently wanted a child, and the mother didn't. She gave the infant to the man, and she vanished. Through intense detective work, Maury eventually located the boy's relatives in the state of Oregon, and they came and got him.

This situation was just the first of many complicated scenarios which surrounded each child and family who were dealing with this disease

8

THE OPENING

We officially opened on November 20, 1988. It was barely 8 months from filing our Articles of Incorporation to opening the doors for childcare. By that time, we had raised $73,000.

Anne Frank wrote in her diary while she was enduring her horrific years of persecution, "How wonderful it is that nobody needs to wait a single minute before starting to improve the world." Thankfully, many people did not wait a single moment to pitch in and help do the work to comfort terminally ill children who would have otherwise been destined to live in hospitals or worse places while they endured this awful disease.

We named the home "Bryan's House" in memory of Scott and Lydia's youngest child who was the first child known to have died of perinatally acquired AIDS in the Dallas/Fort Worth area.

The Grand Opening was on a bright sunny Sunday afternoon. We planned a modest event to not attract too much attention, but word got out. The streets were crowded with people arriving, dressed in fashionable attire, all pouring into the backyard for the festivities. Cars lined the streets for miles in the usually quiet neighborhood. The media showed up in droves, surrounding the event with their trucks loaded with equipment and reporters. With camera operators following, the reporters armed with microphones swarmed the event attempting to get a few words from anyone who looked like they were of any relevance. We had not anticipated the opening was going to be a widely celebrated event, especially not as newsworthy as the media thought it was.

I was still trying to keep a low profile until I cultivated a relationship with the neighbors and dissuaded their fears. I frantically pleaded with the reporters to hold off on their coverage until I could educate the surrounding neighbors and make them comfortable with our presence. Not being media savvy, I thought I had a fighting chance, but I was wrong. They did wait to publish their articles, but only until Monday, and then undeniably, the cat was out of the bag. Unbeknownst to me, the media had already interviewed several neighbors before the opening. In an article, a neighbor said "I think it's all right. It's good for everybody. It doesn't bother me at all." Another neighbor who was interviewed said "This is great, and I wish my children could go over there and help and be with those kids. They need help, and I want to help. I hope they'll let us help. Those children need love." In the end, I was hugely relieved. The neighbors were aware of what we were doing, and so far, they had no objections. Another potentially disastrous issue averted!

On opening day, it was time for me to keep the second of two promises Lydia asked me to make early on: The first was for me to keep her HIV status a secret from everyone while we were working on accomplishing our vision, and the second was when we opened the doors of Bryan's House she could step back into the shadows of anonymity and limit her involvement. The persecution of people with AIDS was at its height, and Lydia feared the high visibility of Bryan's House might compromise her son Matthew's safety. It was also becoming apparent Lydia, and her son's health was deteriorating, and her energy was decreasing. It was time for her to be less involved in Bryan's House and devote the time she had left to her family.

I was on my own. I was losing my collaborator, my friend, and my medical advisor. All along I knew that time would come, it was inevitable, but when it happened, it was a very lonely feeling. As always, Maury was still by my side every step of the way, but the day to day responsibility of caring for the fragile little lives was solely mine.

The entire time my attention was on establishing Bryan's House, the synagogue generously continued to pay my salary and give me the time to do what I needed to accomplish my vision. I officially left my position at the synagogue when we opened and became the full-time Executive Director of Bryan's House. Full time meant, every waking hour. Once again, I gave up earning money to follow my heart. I refrained from taking a salary for quite a long time until I hired all the critical staff and was confident I could cover all our necessary expenses.

It was finally time to actually start rescuing kids! We were licensed as a "Foster Group Home" with space to care for nine children at one time. We were about to embark on providing medically managed day care, respite care and residential care for children ages 0 to 11 affected by HIV/AIDS. When we opened our doors 27 women and children, were immediately in need of services. 9 were adults who were infected, and 5 were infected children. The remainder were uninfected children whose parents were too sick to care for them. The five infected children were our priority which initially only left four spaces available to juggle the thirteen uninfected kids. The four spaces left immediately became inadequate for the uninfected children who needed care when their parent was hospitalized or too ill to take care of them. After all the work which had been done, turning children away who needed care, was frustrating.

Our survival was heavily dependent on our volunteers. They came from every walk of life. People from the LGBTQ community, men and women from every ethnicity, individuals, and organizations. Each having their own personal reason for reaching out to these children. Many brave people pushed past their fears to do whatever was needed to help with the children. There were also many who couldn't push past their concerns, but they did want to help, so they donated goods, services, and money. And then there were those who stayed away because they blamed the parent's behavior for putting their children in this tragic situation.

Many volunteers anticipated that being with these children would be sad and depressing, but it was quite the opposite. The atmosphere which prevailed inside the doors of the home was cheerful and upbeat. Most of the children were too young to be aware they were sick and dying. Once most volunteers walked through the doors and saw the smiling faces, they were hooked and any fear they had dissolved away, and they loved the children as if they were their own.

For some volunteers, it became an intense commitment to a particular family, a child or to the organization itself. It was not unusual for a volunteer to make a lifelong commitment to a family or child. One such relationship was when we were put in contact with a family living outside of the Dallas area. Mother, father, and an infant were infected, and they also had three uninfected children. They were isolated and had no one to turn to for help. Our nurse, Mary Mallory, made the long trek to assess the situation and see what we could do to help. The baby was failing to survive his fight for life. The parents did not have the knowledge or the strength to medically care for the baby and he was on the brink of death. Mary brought him back to Bryan's House for temporary care to provide lifesaving medical intervention. She made the commitment to his family that he would be returned to them as soon as his health improved. The family was extremely grateful. The baby was half the size of a baby of his age. His little arms and legs dangled lifelessly. Ellen Osburn, a volunteer, was drawn to this baby who had big blue eyes, compelling her to commit herself to this baby and his family for as long as they lived. She became their saving grace. She was there to meet the families every need. They would frequently call her and say, "He's really sick, come get him" and Ellen would respond immediately. She would bring him back to Bryan's House and Mary would treat him until he was better and then Ellen would reunite him with his parents. After the baby's death and then the father's death, Ellen continued to maintain constant support to the remaining family who suffered this unimaginable tragedy even providing them with a headstone for the baby's grave. Ellen is one of the shining examples of the depth of relationships which Bryan's house facilitated.

A never anticipated benefit of the initial plan was the children's exposure to volunteers or staff who fell in love with a particular child and welcomed them into their own families. For some of the children who were orphaned, either due to abandonment or the death of parents, a special connection developed between the child and the volunteer or staff person and they adopted the child. Childless parents found children they were longing for and children found forever families who despite the child's background, were willing to give them a permanent home.

Volunteers were our lifeline. Early on, one of the first organizations which reached out to provide manpower, was the Junior League of Dallas. They provided a badly needed, constant flow, of assistance. Some even became permanent staff members and longtime committed volunteers. Nancy Roe became the liaison between the Junior League and Bryan's House. Initially she arrived with much trepidation. Before she made her first visit, she researched the limited information which was available about the contagious nature of HIV/AIDS. Like so many volunteers who reached out to help, Nancy's compassion outweighed her fears. It took courage to walk through the doors when little was known about this mysterious disease. To this day, Nancy and a handful of others are still actively committed to the mission of Bryan's House.

Always, amongst many of the other volunteers, Maury, Kim, Josh and my parents were my faithful helpers. They never denied my call for help and always gave their all. They painted, cleaned, gardened, changed diapers, took care of the children and did anything which needed to be done. Kim and Josh, being teenagers and involved in typical teenager activity, never once objected to answering my call for help. It molded their personalities and contributed to them becoming the caring human beings who they are today.

Maury a busy attorney, tirelessly worked on everything I needed him for. He was my champion when it came to all the legal and diplomatic issues at Bryan's House. I had a mission to accomplish and very little inclination to focus on diplomacy. He was the consummate diplomat and I wasn't. His charm was irresistible when it came to advocate for the children. In retrospect, I wish I had been more tactful in some situations, but fortunately Maury would step in to fill that role when necessary. He was my sounding board when I needed an objective opinion. I could always trust he would be honest with me, unlike other people who were influenced by their own agenda. He'd dry my tears of frustration and build me up to overcome the obstacles. Someone once asked Maury what his proudest accomplishment in life was. His answer was "Helping Stefanie to accomplish great things." He was truly the wind beneath my wings.

Maury served as Chairman of the Board from the inception until August 1988. He stepped down because he was concerned it might appear there was a conflict of interest because we were married. He felt it would be in the corporation's best interest to elect a new Chairman in light of the relationship between us. He remained on the Board and enlisted his friend Tom Higier, Attorney, to serve as Chairman.

Dorothy (Lindsay's grandmother and a participant in the original support group), volunteered from the start without hesitation. She was an invaluable surrogate mother to every child who we cared for. Combined with her loving care, her ability to manage every aspect of running a household, was faultless. While I was feverishly working on getting the facility licensed and up and running, I was afforded complete confidence the children were being well cared for. She cooked and cleaned and was relentless in trying to take care of me. When I was too busy working to stop and eat, she would make meals of my favorite foods and then stay and insist I take time out to eat. With all the losses in her life and the stress she was dealing with on a daily basis trying to keep Lindsay healthy, she still managed to put her heart and soul into caring for every child who entered the doors of the house.

Dorothy multi-tasking with the children.

It was a group effort. Everyone involved pitched in to do whatever needed to be done, even if it wasn't their assigned roll. Staff and volunteers did office work, cared for the children, cleaned house and consoled crying babies. Having contact with the children was always the highlight of my day.

The search for funds was never ending. Emotionally, I constantly vacillated between feeling confident the funding would work out, to feelings of doubt we were going to be able to meet the ongoing needs of the infected. The increasing number of families and children in need, were becoming more and more evident. It was imperative to cover the existing expenses, but it was also important to consider our future needs. We were never in the red and I never spent a dime we didn't have in the bank. Some funds were considered designated funds which meant they could only be spent on what the donor had intended them for. It was a difficult balance to keep. Sometimes our balance sheet looked great, but it was because the funds we had received had been designated to be spent on particular expenses leaving us little money to purchase the daily necessities. The budget continuously needed a watchful eye to ensure our daily needs were met and we could survive long term.

At the beginning, all the grants which we applied for were from private funders as opposed to state or federal grants. The City of Dallas announced that they had created demonstration grants which were available to assist AIDS service providers. Unfamiliar with the process, I researched what it would take to qualify for the funds and immediately pursued the opportunity. I was not going to let any source of funding pass me by. The parameters of a demonstration grant were ideal for us because they were open to start up organizations. The grants were awarded on the basis of innovative programs which were promising and worthwhile. The city was at a loss on how they were going to provide services for people with AIDS, so they created demonstration grants to assist organizations. The grants provided funding to organizations who were on the forefront of providing services. To request funding from the grant, I had to present the need for the funds to the city council. Again, I was concerned the lack of verifiable numbers of families and children in need would disqualify us, but I had nothing to lose so I went for it. At first, the process was somewhat intimidating because I had never even been to a City Council meeting and the entire process was unfamiliar to me. The auditorium appeared huge to me. The city council sat at the front in their designated seats. A podium with a microphone on it stood in front of the council members, and behind it was many elevated rows of seats with all the existing AIDS service providers clamoring for the same pot of money. I went armed with all the material and the talking points I might need to make our case and walked away with a commitment of $75,000. Getting the grant was a huge reinforcement to my confidence that we just might be able to survive and meet future needs.

The first federal grant we applied for ended up being a disaster. Naively, we had joined with the People with AIDS Coalition on a partner grant. The PWA Coalition, changed their name and is now named AIDS Services of Dallas. The Coalition provided housing for adults with HIV/AIDS and we were providing housing for children, so it seemed like it was a natural fit for the grant requirements. They were anxious to partner with us because they felt they would have a better chance of being approved because there were children involved. The grant was approved, and we briefly felt some financial security because the funding was for two years. The relief was short lived. Being inexperienced in the federal grant process, Lydia and I gave the coalition all our information to apply for the grant and they took the lead in the application process. When the grant was awarded, we found out we had been deceived. To qualify for the funds, the grant stipulated Bryan's House would have to move our location to the same location as the PWA Coalition. Even though we were desperate for the funds we declined to participate in the funding. We had just completed the existing home and were licensed only at our existing site. Also, the Coalition was located in a part of town which was not desirable for volunteers to go to and we were heavily volunteer dependent. In addition, we needed to be near the hospital complex, and they weren't. It was one of the many learning experiences along the way.

As the never-ending stress of staying financially solvent persisted we continued to be constantly defending that there were enough children with AIDS to justify the amount of money it would take to sustain the home. Again, the doubters were nipping at our heals. We were in the trenches trying to care of as many children as we could, and our numbers were growing daily. The gay community had so many more adults who were infected, and we were all fighting for the same dollars. It was a constant battle to justify what we were doing. The women and children were in desperate need of help in spite of the fact they were fewer in number.

9

FLOURISHING

Once we were open, I woke up each morning immediately thinking about the many things I had to get done that day. Fraught with challenges, the real all-encompassing work began. Maury and I would lie in bed brainstorming. Tossing ideas back and forth which gave me clarity on what the priorities of the day would be. My mind would be busy planning while we were getting ready for work and then, as always, we would ride to work together. Riding together minimized the time we had to be apart. Sounds obsessive to most but being together was what made us both the happiest. At the end of the workday, whoever had the car would pick up the other, and most days we would meet friends and go out for the evening. I had a little more trouble ending my work day than Maury did. There was always one more thing to do. On days I was picking up Maury, Dorothy became my boss. She would stay on me until I walked out the door. When I needed a little more time to work, she was vigilant in prodding me out the door, all the while saying things like "Maury's waiting for you. Now don't you keep him waiting" or "that stuff can wait till morning, you don't want to make Maury mad now." Maury rarely got mad about anything, but I appreciated her watching out for Maury's best interest and mine too.

Every morning when I arrived at the house on Knight Street, I couldn't help being enveloped by happiness. It wasn't because of the satisfaction of the accomplishment; it was the pure joy I felt seeing the busy, cheerful environment with children laughing and playing oblivious to an illness which was killing them. In spite of sickness and death looming over the house, on the surface, it appeared all was well. The people who volunteered had to have a lot of love in their hearts to put aside their sadness and make every child's day their very best day.

The AIDS virus remained a mystery. Many unanswered questions about the transmission and treatment of the disease continued. In March of 1987, the drug Azidothymidine (AZT) became approved for the treatment of adults with AIDS. It was the first drug approved which showed promise in treating symptoms and potentially extending life. In May of 1990 AZT was finally approved for use in children.

The opening was only the beginning of the many obstacles to overcome. Focusing on keeping sick children as well as possible was a demanding priority for everyone involved and we were doing a good job at it. Doctors involved in their care were skeptical at first in our ability to provide out of hospital health care, but it wasn't long before we proved our attentive care was extending the lives of these doomed children. An article by Ashley Cheshire in the Fort Worth Star Telegram read "In the sense that magic is always an illusion, there is an acknowledged magic about Bryan's House." Accolades were abundant.

The numbers of children needing help was becoming overwhelming. As soon as we opened, we needed more space. Every child who we could not accommodate was a heartbreaker. We were juggling kids, prioritizing who was in the most need of care each day. Almost from the start, the need for expansion loomed.

The constant search for funding was always an ongoing struggle. Initially, our finances were tenuous, but as time went on, and funding came in, we began to have confidence that we would survive. We were receiving some daily funding from the state for the resident children who were in the custody of DHS and that afforded us a source of some ongoing funding for their care. All of our services, including childcare, were free to the families and children. In the beginning, our total expenditures per month, to cover the cost of our overhead and a few paid staff, was $6,631. Donated goods and services covered all other expenses. Amazingly, the finances seemed in pretty good shape for our present needs, but the looming cost of expansion was never far from my thoughts.

As the number of children increased, child care staff became the most significant expense. DHS required one staff person for every four children. Although it was not mandatory, ideally, I wanted two paid staff and one trained volunteer for every four children. My requirement of extra staff and volunteers was essential in making sure every child was receiving the best of care.

By December 1988, we had raised $73,724, and an additional $112,604 was approved but not yet received. From the beginning of our pursuit of funds, six grants had been denied. In December we were waiting to hear from funders on an additional $686,815.

Although many in the gay community felt threatened by our ability to raise money, as time went on, they began to see our value in the bigger picture. Eventually, the existing service organizations began to realize they were not equipped to deal with the emerging challenges of women and children. Our benefit to them became apparent when the Resource Center found themselves in the predicament of not knowing what to do with the 8-year-old boy whose surrogate dad was dying. Our assistance with the boy was the turning point in our relationship with those in the gay community who were vehemently opposed to our existence. Some in the gay community even began to raise money for our cause. People were holding parties and events constantly to help the gay community, and Bryan's House began to get a portion of the funds. Maury and I were well known and well liked in the gay community, so when I had a need which the gay community could help with, doors were open to us. There were often unexpected expenses along the way, and the assistance from these fundraisers was invaluable.

Every day there were hoops to jump through and problems to be solved. The little rays of sunshine from the generosity of people helped me believe all was going to be okay. Christmas looked bleak for the many families who were now contacting us for help. Our families were dealing with so much, and I wanted them to have a joyous Christmas even though this dark cloud was hanging over their heads. I spread the word that we needed gifts and Christmas trees with all the embellishments. The donations started arriving in truckloads. The house began filling up with gifts and trees galore. We barely had enough room for our daily needs and no extra storage to accommodate the massive amounts of donations. We couldn't distribute the gifts fast enough, and we were becoming overwhelmed. I needed to solve this fantastic problem quickly! Once again it took "out of the box thinking" to figure out a solution. I contacted a trucking company and persuaded them to let us borrow the bed of an 18-wheeler, which they were not using, so we could store the Christmas items. I then got permission from the owners of the vacant property next door to park it on their empty lot. Within days the first truck was filled to the brim. Again, I contacted the trucking company, and they brought me a second one. The grateful families had the Christmas of their dreams.

For quite a while we could only afford a minimum of paid staff. Initially, the staff consisted of caretakers for the children and eventually a full-time nurse. I had the ultimate responsibility every day, 24 hours a day, for the health and well-being of every child in our care. Once the house opened, it was ultimately on me to supervise the care of the children and keep them safe and as healthy as possible. Also, I had to oversee support services to the families, raise and manage funds, supervise staff and volunteers and problem solve the many issues which came along. There was hardly ever enough time to stop and think about the enormity of it all. My greatest pleasure was to take a break from all the administrative responsibilities and hold a baby or play with a toddler or make a child smile. It was not an unusual site to see me writing a grant while comforting a child on my lap. Amongst the chaos and the frustration of worrying about money and being overwhelmed with complete exhaustion, all it took was for me to pause and remember I was doing all this to give a quality of life to these dying children and it would rejuvenate me. Of utmost importance to me was no child, suffering from this despicable disease, was ever deprived of the loving care most children have. My biggest frustration continued to be turning down children in need of care because of our limited capacity.

The day to day programming was in constant flux. The massively complicated needs of this population became apparent as we went along. I had to continually evaluate the programs we had in place to make sure we were meeting the ever-changing needs of the children and families. Providing a support group for fathers was a program which we had not recognized initially. These men were dealing with being left with children to care for when their wives were too ill or had died from the disease. Often, they were sick themselves, and many times they were caring for their sick children. The support groups in existence, for adult gay males, did not address the kinds of problems which fathers were dealing with.

There became a need to create a program for uninfected preschoolers whose parents were infected. These children were typically excluded from attending school because of the stigma and fear associated with being from a family who had AIDS. Therefore, we needed to implement an early education program.

Another need we had not anticipated was a support group for uninfected women who were in a relationship with an infected man and infected women who were dating. Programming was in constant flux. New programs were implemented as the need arose and others were eliminated if it became apparent they were not of value. It was a continual balance of trial and error.

The most important aspect of our program was focusing on keeping the kids well, every ounce a child gained was cause for celebration. Every sneeze or a cough signaled action because it could be life-threatening. Every child had their unique vulnerabilities, and absolutely nothing could be overlooked, because if it was, it could hasten their death. There was always a bit of hope that if we could keep these children alive until the medical community came up with treatment for them, they might have a chance to live. The attentive and dedicated nurses took care of every child as if they were their own.

Each child in care had different needs. The only common denominator was they had HIV/AIDS, or their parents were infected. Each child came with their own unique story and health issues. For many, Bryan's House became the only support they could rely on during the lowest point in their life.

Cassie, the first resident to permanently live at Bryan's House, was four years old. She had AIDS and had spent her life in a Galveston, Texas Hospital. Galveston Child Protective Services (CPS) requested placement for her at Bryan's House. All the information we had was there was a child with AIDS who had multiple disabilities who needed some place to live. She was denied admission to foster homes and nursing facilities. Before meeting her, we had no idea we were about to encounter a child with many severe disabilities and life-threatening medical problems in addition to having AIDS.

With much trepidation, nurse Mary Mallory and I boarded a plane to fly to Galveston to evaluate Cassie and see if we thought we could provide the kind of care she needed. Our first observation when we entered Cassie's hospital room was of a frightened little girl peering through the bars of a metal hospital crib. There was a top on the crib, so she couldn't fall or climb out which made it look like she was caged. My first impression was, this very sick, unfortunate little girl was in desperate need of a loving environment. This little girl's appearance was disturbing. She had no voice, and her cry was silent. Cassie's face was contorted with one eye more prominent than the other, and her eyes were set unusually far apart. She had an endless stream of secretions coming from her nose and mouth. When we approached, to try and pick her up, she was like a wild animal, spitting and flailing her arms and legs. It was her only means of communication, and she anticipated anyone who was touching her was there to administer medical treatment. When we tried to touch her, she would recoil and cry this silent cry which could only be recognized by the anguish on her face. She was the saddest child I had ever seen.

Cassie was born to a 16-year-old Caucasian unwed mother who was unable to take care of her. She was born with a genetic defect called Charge Syndrome. Charge Syndrome is an extremely complex syndrome which causes extensive medical and physical difficulties. Cassie had been subjected to multiple surgeries in her short life, and as a result, contracted HIV/AIDS through a blood transfusion. Her disabilities were extensive. We were informed she was deaf, visually impaired, unable to walk or speak and had severe pulmonary problems. She was also labeled severely retarded. She could not swallow food and had to be fed through a tube in her stomach. She suffered from high fevers and constant diarrhea. Her medical care was very complicated. She lived in isolation from most personal contact except from the people who were giving her medical care, a rare visit from her mother and one devoted volunteer. The volunteer, Bobby Dotson, gave Cassie the only unconditional love she received in her lonely life while she was in the hospital. She was living her life as a lonely caged human. She was frightened of people, and any attempt to console her was met with a violent tantrum. Hospital personal informed us they thought she would not live more than a month. It was a sad scenario, and I was compelled to give her the care and love she deserved even if it was for the limited time we thought she had left to live.

I knew excepting this child into Bryan's House was our most significant challenge to date and one I had not anticipated. We would have the responsibility for the life of this child, and it was terrifying. I never imagined the first permanent resident to live at the house would be this medically compromised. I could not stand the thought of not accepting her. Her only alternative would be to live the rest of her life in these unacceptable circumstances. Mary doubted my judgment when I decided to accept Cassie for care at Bryan's House. She was very concerned about whether or not we could adequately deal with Cassie's multitude of medical problems. More than me, she fully understood the scope of the ramifications of my decision to bring her back to Bryan's House. Mary was basing her concerns on reason and medical knowledge, and I was listening to my heart.

I called Maury from my hotel room that night before we were to transport Cassie from the hospital to Dallas. I told him "it was going to be hard, but I felt I had to do it." I was sure I could make a difference in this little one's life. Her medical needs, her uncivilized behavior, her spitting, the inability to communicate with her and her temper tantrums were going to be a challenge. I asked Maury to find an old-fashioned wood playpen and fashion a lid on it. My thought was, at least initially, it would be a more familiar transition for her. Maury was not adept at building things but, of course, he did it. Taking Cassie from the only environment she was familiar with was going to be traumatic for her and we had to sedate her for the plane ride to Dallas.

I also had concerns about our ability to care for Cassie, but I couldn't give up on this lost little sole and I was determined to improve her quality of life. I was fully cognizant that it was going to be an intensely serious challenge to keep her well, especially for Mary. Before even leaving Galveston, I had made arrangements for the Visiting Nurse Association (VNA) to assist us in her care when we arrived in Dallas. I previously had applied for a grant which would cover the costs of their backup assistance if we needed additional medical help and they became invaluable in the care of Cassie. Together with the VNA, Mary's outstanding medical supervision, and everyone's patience and love, we managed to keep Cassie healthier and happier beyond anyone's expectations.

Cassie required at least ten diaper changes a day because of her constant diarrhea. Initially, she had to be fed every two hours through a tube protruding from her stomach. She required six breathing treatments a day which included suctioning to keep her airways clear. After not too long Cassie began to thrive at Bryan's House. Little by little she made strides. She started to tolerate being held and amazingly learned to smile and laugh. It became apparent her deficits were not as severe as we were initially told, and the predictions of her life expectancy were wrong. The drug AZT had not been approved for use in children yet, but we were able to get her into a clinical trial which allowed her to receive it and it vastly improved her health. We began to recognize her deafness was not as much of a physical deficit as it was her way of shutting out the world. She appeared to have enough sight to manage some tasks. Like many of her problems, her supposedly severe retardation was not as bad as we were originally told. It was likely the severity of her mental deficits was a result of her lack of stimulation and deprivation from living her life in the hospital. We worked very hard on trying to normalize her life as much as possible. We attempted to acclimate her to the taste of food, so she could get rid of the feeding tube and eat by mouth. Dorothy, the master at getting a child to eat, worked with her continuously. Unfortunately, we didn't have any success with all our many efforts of trying to feed her, so we had her examined by a specialist and found out her stomach had been altered and it was physically impossible for her to eat. We suspected a feeding tube had been inserted because it was easier to feed her that way in the hospital. We tried to get it reversed but were advised her medical condition was too fragile to do the surgery which was needed to correct the problem. It seemed too risky for a child who we were told did not have long to live.

Cassie had one highlight in her life before moving her to Bryan's House. Bobby Dotson, Cassie's faithful volunteer caretaker, who was a 56-year-old former policeman. He had heard about Cassie from a secretary at his credit union who told him about a little girl who was living in the hospital who rarely had visitors. When she was in Galveston, Bobby visited her every night after work, and the bond between the two became Cassie's lifeline. He became her advocate. Bobby rattled a lot of cages on her behalf and a lot of times was labeled as an irritant to the hospital personnel and CPS who had custody of her. He was faithful to his commitment in trying to get the best possible care for Cassie. When CPS informed Bobby they were moving her to Bryan's House, he thought they were trying to split the duo up, so he would no longer be able to cause them problems. He vigorously fought the move because he thought they were sending her to a nursing home where she would not get the care or attention which he insisted she should have. He took CPS to court to obtain authority over her care and lost. Initially, being separated was a devastating blow to them both. After Cassie was moved to Bryan's House, Bobby flew up to Dallas every weekend to visit her. As time passed, and Bobby recognized the new life we had given her, he became grateful that Cassie finally had a loving home.

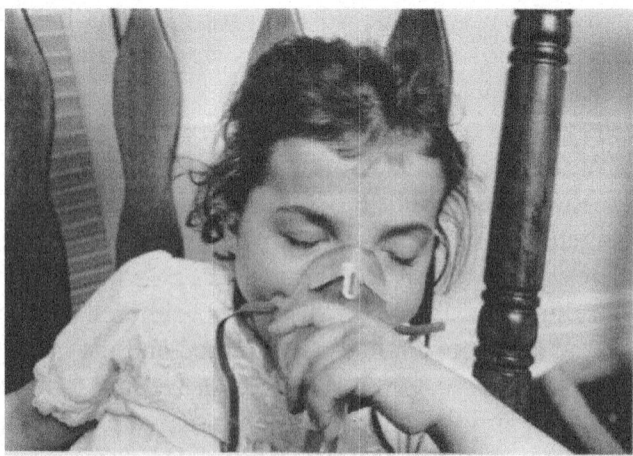

Cassie sleeping through one of her many medical treatments.

The ability to meet Cassie's medical needs and improve her quality of life affirmed our credibility to those in the medical community who had doubts about whether we could competently care for just about any child with complex medical needs.

Beth was born at the end of December 1988 to an 18-year-old African American mother who was infected with HIV after sharing IV drug needles. During pregnancy, Beth's mother's antibodies were transferred from her to her fetus, and as in all newborns born to infected mothers, Beth tested HIV positive at birth. The doctor treating Beth and the CPS social worker determined her mother was not competent to take care of Beth. Beth became a ward of the state, and her destiny was she would live out her life in the hospital until it was determined whether or not she was truly infected with AIDS. At the time, it could take up to two years old to determine whether or not a newborn had indeed contracted HIV from their mother or the test was reflecting the mother's immune system. About 30% to 60% of newborns born to HIV positive mothers would actually be infected with HIV. Beth was born at Parkland Memorial Hospital, which was the county hospital, and lived there until she was admitted to Bryan's House. Before the availability of Bryan's House, Beth would have remained in the hospital until it was confirmed she did not have the disease, and only then would she be eligible for foster care or adoption. At six weeks old she was placed at Bryan's House. Beth appeared to be as healthy as any newborn except that she was suffering from withdrawal symptoms from the drugs her mother had taken while she was pregnant. Many of the infants came to us with withdrawal symptoms as a result of their mother's drug use. Infants born to drug-addicted mothers most often had to go through withdrawal. Out of necessity, the staff learned ways to comfort babies through their withdrawal symptoms. Lots of TLC and holding, rocking, and limiting the activity around them helped. Through trial and error, we figured out methods to ease their pain. We discovered if we put a drug-addicted infant, in an infant seat, and placed them on top of a running dryer, the motion would often comfort them.

Beth was an exquisite baby. Underweight at birth, she had tiny little perfect features. Beth looked like an artist's rendering of a perfect little doll. Her brown curly hair and her flawless complexion contributed to her classic looks, and she was appealing to everyone. I fell in love with her from the first day I brought her home from the hospital. Maury and my kids also fell in love with her, as did anyone who had contact with her. Maury and I had many discussions about adopting her ourselves which was a bit crazy considering how much I was already doing but the love for this little girl outweighed reason. The only issue which gave us pause was that it might be better for her to live in an African American home. Our first choice for her was to be adopted by someone in her culture, but if it were not possible, we would adopt her and make every effort to keep her heritage alive in her life. As an infant, she was by my side as I worked and often went home with me when possible. As she got older and was participating in activities with the other children, she would go to Dorothy and demand she be taken to my office. Under Dorothy's watchful eye she would toddle across the play yard to my office and bang on my door. No matter how busy I was, I always had time for her.

Beth with her eternal smile.

Sharon was eight years old when she was admitted to Bryan's House. She was very ill due to a failed kidney transplant and her neglectful drug-addicted mother was not taking her to her life-sustaining daily dialysis treatments. In addition to her kidney disease, Sharon had contracted HIV through a transfusion during her transplant surgery. One fourth of her life was spent in hospitals and she was dependent on daily dialysis to keep her alive. She was a gutsy little girl who all alone would convince bus drivers to take her to Children's Medical Center to get her dialysis treatments. When social workers at CMC became aware that her neglectful mother was not adequately taking care of her, they contacted Child Protective Services who found it imperative to remove her from her mother's custody. Because of her HIV status there was no alternative placement for her, and she was going to have to live her life in the hospital. When CPS requested placement at Bryan's House, we knew her complex medical needs were going to be a challenge, but with no satisfactory alternatives for placement elsewhere, we accepted her as a permanent resident. This little girl had spent her life coping with unimaginable trauma and neglect and we were determined to figure out how to give this child a better life. Before her life at Bryan's House, her life had been continuously disrupted from countless hospital stays and daily dialysis. She was unable to attend school or have any interaction with other children, but with attentive care she had the potential to lead a more normal life in spite of her illness. At Bryan's House, Sharon was able to feel cared for, and the attentive nursing care was able to minimize her hospital stays. We learned how to administer her life-saving dialysis treatments during the night at the house which enabled her to attend school during the day. Living at Bryan's House, Sharon's quality of life changed dramatically, and this little 8-year-old girl no longer had to care for herself.

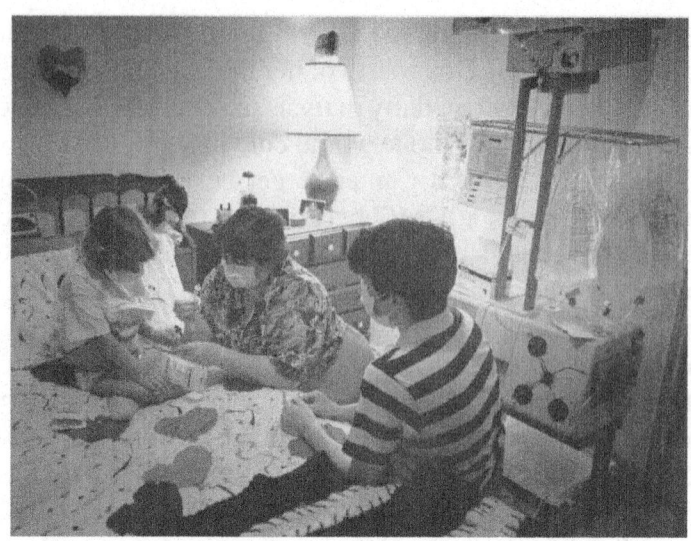

Sharon receiving her nightly dialysis treatments.

Angela abandoned at birth, was born to a drug-addicted mother with Syphilis and AIDS. She was born with an underdeveloped brain as a result of the Syphilis, and her prognosis for the future was grim. She weighed less than average at birth and was unresponsive to the world around her. Angela failed to thrive and remained tiny even though the one thing she could do was suck on a bottle with vigor. At one year old she weighed only 10 pounds. Her big dark eyes appeared lifeless and hollow. Her cry was silent and only if one was paying close attention, could you recognize she was crying. There was something special about this tiny little girl who compelled volunteers to fall in love with her in spite of the fact she was barely responsive. Occasionally, with a lot of cajoling, a smile might appear on her face. Her smile would light up the room and would be celebrated by all.

One night, Patsy and her baby Jennifer showed up on our doorstep with nowhere to go. They were homeless and tested positive to the virus. Licensing prohibited adult clients to stay overnight but it would have been unconscionable to turn this duo away, so we made an exception. We embraced this young woman and provided her with a support system which she had never had throughout her entire life. The first challenge was to find her a cost-free, permanent place to live. My friend Don Maison, the Executive Director at AIDS Services of Dallas (ASD), took pity on our pleas and bypassed the usual waiting list and excepted Patsy and her daughter Jennifer for emergency placement. It was a place where they could live amongst infected people who would except and nurture them. Through donations, we provided her with all the essentials she needed to have a quality life. During the day, Jennifer would come to Bryan's House for daycare and often stayed overnight when her mother wasn't well enough to care for her. Her mother Patsy, an orphan herself, was all alone in the world. She had been living on the streets and working for a pimp when she found out she was pregnant. During her prenatal exam, at ten weeks gestation, she was informed she was infected with the AIDS virus. Patsy was told about the possible ramifications the virus could have on her unborn child, and she was urged to have an abortion. She chose not to abort the only living family she would ever have. She couldn't explain why she decided to keep her child; her only explanation was "she gives me hope." Jennifer, like all other infants born to an infected mother, tested HIV positive at birth. She was an exceptionally happy newborn who appeared healthy from the start despite testing positive to HIV.

Patsy's health deteriorated fairly rapidly, and when she was well enough, she was able to live a contented life with her baby. The mainly gay residents at ASD welcomed her with open arms and helped her to care for Jennifer. Patsy finally had an extended family which excepted her for who she was. Grateful for a home, Patsy would work the switchboard at ASD when she felt okay. When Patsy suffered bouts of illness which disabled her, Jennifer would be cared for at Bryan's House for as long as needed. The goal was to unite mother and baby whenever possible. With Bryan's House support, mother and child were able to stay intact as a family. At seven months, Jennifer miraculously began testing negative and remained negative in subsequent tests. After suffering through a lonely life herself, the most important thing to Patsy was that when she died, her baby would have a family. A couple who were faithful volunteers at Bryan's House fell in love with this beautiful little girl, and they made a pledge to Patsy that they would adopt Jennifer when Patsy could no longer care for her. From that moment on, the adopting family, lovingly included Patsy in their family's life until the day she died. She left this earth knowing her daughter had, what she never had, a loving family.

A mother and father and a baby boy arrived at Bryan's House one morning. They had been at Parkland Hospital all night seeking medical care because they were homeless and didn't feel well. Ultimately, it was discovered that the cause for their symptoms was the dreaded HIV. Mother, father, and the baby all tested positive to the virus. They had been heavily addicted to heroin and had been battling their addiction for some time. Lacking the knowledge of the risks of sharing needles, they contracted the virus from other infected drug addicts. Their addiction rendered them penniless. They had been shoplifting and working the streets to support their habit and their family. They were new in town and had no resources. The social worker at the hospital referred them to us for help. All they had was the clothes they were wearing and a baby stroller. They had been staying at a motel, but they left there in the dark of the night because they couldn't pay their bill. When they arrived at Bryan's House, we recognized they were in dire straits, and we immediately took them in and came up with a plan of action to help them. They had no resources and no place to stay, but they said they were now motivated to quit their drug habit. Without our intense support, it was unlikely they would be able to sustain their desire to become sober. We provided the items to meet their immediate needs and money to pay for their motel room until we could get them into ASD for housing. They entered a methadone treatment program, and it worked. They had made many attempts to quit and miraculously, this time they were successful, but unfortunately it was too late to avoid becoming infected with AIDS. We kept in very close contact with them, providing them with volunteers who maintained continuous contact to support them in their struggles. After not too long, they were able to get jobs. We provided childcare to their HIV positive baby, so they could work without being concerned their baby was not getting proper medical care. For us, it was a fantastic success story. The little boy eventually became HIV negative and continued to receive daycare at Bryan's House while his parents worked. With our constant support to this family, we were successful in changing their destiny.

Women, children, and entire families came to us for help from every walk of life, every ethnicity, every socio-economic class and every unique set of circumstances. What they all had in common was they or their family member was dying. Our arms and our hearts were always open no matter what the circumstances were. No one was ever turned away or charged anything for the help which Bryan's House provided. Compassion without judgment was abundant for all who walked through the doors.

Volunteers came to Bryan's House with a dedication which was inspiring and selfless. Long lasting relationships were built, in life and for those who were left behind. The far-reaching impact on families which Bryan's House facilitated can never be quantified. Every volunteer who gave of themselves gained a lasting perspective on life which will carry them through their own trials and tribulations.

Bryan's House created the illusion that all was okay under the roof on Knight Street. Children in their pretty little outfits, playing and laughing with loving caretakers responding to their every need. To the bystander, all was well until they looked a little closer and noticed the medical equipment, the numerous boxes of gloves and surgical masks, the bleach stations for containing bodily fluids and the garbage compactors for waste disposal. Looking closer, a bystander could not ignore the hideous realization that most of these gravely ill children were dying.

The daily life for the infected children appeared somewhat like any other child's typical day except for intermittent healthcare intervention. My overall philosophy for these dying children was to do everything possible to keep them happy. The necessary training, in a well child's life, was irrelevant in the infected children's lives. Toilet training, preparing them for school and other activities which would cause them stress was not a priority. In contrast, the children who were well or had the potential of becoming HIV negative, the focus was on skills they needed to live a normal life. In either situation, the primary focus was to provide these children, who were suffering the cruel effects of being affected by AIDS, a life that was surrounded by love and contentment.

I will never know if it was the attentive medical care or the loving care or both, but every child who came through the doors far exceeded the statistics of the life expectancies of children living with AIDS.

As this mystery disease went on many of the unanswered questions were figured out, but there continued to be a lack of information about the long-term effects of the disease in children. There was some data, although not confirmed, that a child born HIV positive, could convert to negative and possibly convert back to positive, but because of the lack of long-term studies it could not be definitively determined. Dr. Richard Wasserman, who specialized in pediatric immune deficiencies, and a Temple Emanu-El member, faithfully sat on the board of Open Arms, Inc. from the start. One of the pioneers in pediatric HIV/AIDS, he took care of many of our kids. He said in an article in The Dallas Times Herald, "There are no guarantees of anything. There have been a few cases, four in Italy and one in Baltimore, where a child was initially positive, then repeatedly tested negative and after several years showed up positive and developed the disease." The lack of definitive data continued to mystify the medical community throughout the epidemic and to this day there are still unanswered questions and no cure.

In 1987, when we began to think about a solution for families and children with HIV/AIDS, Dallas was ranked as the fifth highest county in the United States with cases of women and children with AIDS. As time progressed, many of the infected newborns were more likely being abandoned than nurtured. Even children who eventually converted to being negative were not getting the parental care which they needed and alternative placement remained unavailable.

By March 1989, there were 82 children who we were providing some level of care to. In addition, the number of parents requiring on-site support services was rapidly increasing. As the overall number of infected was continuing to rise, our expenses were growing proportionately.

There was barely time to breathe before thoughts of expansion became a necessity. Cassie, Beth, Sharon, and Angela were permanent overnight residents and the rest of the children in need of care were rotated in and out of daycare and overnight respite care. Lindsay was a permanent daycare client enabling Dorothy to be able to work at Bryan's House while caring for her. Fortunately, DHS allowed us not to include Lindsay in our daily census because Dorothy was there with her. Care for unaffected children, whose parents were infected and too ill to take care of them, ended up being low on the priority list because of the lack of space which DHS had approved. Sadly, children desperately needing attention had to be turned away daily, and it broke our hearts each time we had to decline any child for care. Not surprising to us, the nine spaces which we were approved for were inadequate the day we opened our doors.

Every day the house was alive with activity. Children were playing, volunteers and staff were arriving for their shifts to bathe, dress, feed, change the numerous diapers, and perform any other necessary jobs to keep the house running. The nurses were busy administering ongoing life-sustaining medical treatments and taking the children to their doctors' appointments. Parents came and went for meetings to address their needs and find assistance and solutions which were essential to their circumstances. Newly diagnosed families in distress were arriving continuously for help, all with their own unique set of problems.

10

THE JUGGLING ACT

With a minimum of paid staff, it was difficult to keep up with the administrative work while making sure all the essential activity, pertaining to the children, was being maintained with the highest of standards. As always, funding required constant attention. Researching avenues of donations and exploring possible funding was an ongoing process. The priority became paying for all the essential overhead needed to keep the existing program funded while looking for future funds for the inevitable expansion. Every expenditure was weighed and evaluated to make sure it was a necessity. In addition to the stress of working with very ill children, staff did not have ideal working conditions due to the lack of space and minimal office supplies.

As funding came in, additional staff were hired to supplement the volunteer help. I finally was able to hire staff who were critical to sustaining the house. When grants were received allowing the funding for salaries, I hired people in order of their importance to our needs. I didn't take a salary until after I had enough money to pay every essential staff person who was needed. Expenses were rapidly increasing because of the continuous flow of people needing help which resulted in the need to hire more personnel. Fortunately, grant funding was keeping up with our growing needs.

Dorothy became the house manager and was the first paid staff person who was employed to keep the childcare and house running smoothly. The need for a nurse was immediately a high priority to make sure the children's health was being carefully monitored. Shortly after, I hired paid childcare staff as funds came in so we could have a combination of volunteers and paid childcare staff. Therefore, a volunteer coordinator, to train, supervise and recruit volunteers was an essential component while having limited staff. Lastly, a Director of Development whose job it was to maintain the flow of applications to potential funders emerged as a priority.

The luxury of having hired staff seemed like it would have relieved some of the stress on me, but the added responsibility of supervising staff added to my workload.

Every now and then a little jewel of joy helped me to push on. The gratification of finally being able to pay Dorothy for her dedication to the cause gave me that joy. She said, "This is my place in heaven. Now I have a place to leave her (Lindsay). I haven't had any income for the last two years, so this is my dream come true." She had been isolated and unemployed since she took over the care of Lindsay. Struggling financially, with no options which would allow her to work and take care of Lindsay at the same time was indeed the solution to many of the problems she had.

Learning to function on a strict budget, put a lot of strain on the staff. Some of the team who were committed to the mission gladly took part in finding donated goods for the children and the functioning of the house. Others who were not accustomed to working for a nonprofit, and viewed their position as just a job, were not so willing. They resented functioning fiscally conservative, and they became disgruntled. Frugality was essential to our survival and those who were not dedicated to the mission often caused dissension and often didn't last very long. It was essential that everyone was on the same team for the welfare of the children.

Staff management was difficult for me mainly because I was so busy with all the aspects of running the organization. The structure of the organization was not a traditional workplace, so innovative management was a necessity. The pool of qualified personnel was limited because we were dealing with a disease which many feared. It was my policy not to exclude people who were infected from working at Bryan's House. Making exceptions for them when they were unable to work due to their periodic bouts of illness, complicated scheduling.

Some of the staff had been drawn to Bryan's House out of compassion, but then realized they were ill-equipped to deal with the stress involved in the working environment. Adding to the complexities of personnel issues many of the staff were unpaid volunteers. There were instances of volunteers objecting to following the rules which resulted in conflicts with the paid staff. Staff came and went, but those who stayed were deeply committed to provide the best care possible long-term.

In retrospect, my interactions with the staff could have been more nurturing. I was often so busy I didn't take enough time to put my attention on each staff person and the problems they were encountering in their jobs and their own lives. Dealing with the stress of sick and dying children every day often was overwhelming for staff and volunteers, and often emotions were frayed. Also, for some employees, the insecurity of working for an organization with tentative funding contributed to the stress within the organization.

The office staff had to deal with inadequate office space, moving from one area to another at times to accommodate our services. The house was noisy and crowded with children and volunteers and parents coming and going. Often the office staff had to make do with what had been donated as opposed to being able to buy office supplies they needed to make their jobs easier. Their jobs were difficult in many ways, and I should have been more in tune to their needs while accomplishing our common goal.

Many of the staff had no inkling of the overall picture which dictated the use of our resources. Much of the time I felt like I was standing on an island surrounded by people shooting darts at me. I felt if I didn't duck or move side to side quickly, I wouldn't be able to avoid getting hit with the darts and the mission would crumble.

Ultimately, it was my sole responsibility to make sure we had enough money to keep the organization thriving. Also, the thoughts of the inevitable need for expansion made it mandatory we stretch every dollar as far as we could. We had barely been open four months before I had to confront the fact, I needed to focus on a plan which would allow us to accommodate more children.

In the beginning, my intention was to help some children and families in need. After opening, it quickly became apparent that I had the ultimate responsibility to keep the organization, which was growing in leaps and bounds, afloat. I was leading an organization with many facets which needed my intense attention at all times.

I had to be innovative with each new situation because there weren't any models to follow. My lack of experience often became my strength, requiring me to think outside of the box during challenging situations. Steve Jobs words "Innovation distinguishes between a leader and a follower" is a statement which I believe is the guiding light of leadership.

Managing the day to day budget is a complex balancing act. Funding sources, in the nonprofit sector, often designate their funds to be spent on specific expenses. Government funding is particularly challenging because of the strict requirements. To qualify for grant money, most times the government mandates participation in programs and data gathering which are somewhat outside the organization's mission. Deciding whether or not a particular grant is worth adjusting the program to accommodate the requirements, meant weighing the pros and cons carefully and not being blinded by the prospect of money. All grants had to be documented and strictly adhered to. Funds which were not designated for a particular use were a valuable commodity because they enabled us to pay for items which were typically not covered under most grants. We were inconstant need of household items like soap, toilet paper, light bulbs, cleaning products and everything else it took to function and generally grants did not cover these expenses. Undesignated funds were always a bonus so we could pay for the day to day living expenses.

Occasionally, an unsolicited donation would come in from an unexpected source, and it would feel like a gift from heaven. It was often unknown what the donor's motivation was, but it always felt like a little sparkle of light in the ongoing struggle to keep the organization viable. One such instance came on a Saturday morning. I was at home when I got a call from a person who did not want to identify himself. He only told me he was from Canada and wanted to take a tour of Bryan's House on that day. His urgency made me somewhat apprehensive. It was one of the few days I took off, and I was exhausted, but I agreed to meet him. There were several caretakers and volunteers at the house, so I wasn't concerned for my safety, but it did feel kind of unsettling to meet a stranger who sounded intently urgent. When I answered the door, there was a very nicely dressed man, who did not want to have a lot of conversation, so I just took his lead and walked him around the house.

As he was ready to leave, he casually handed me a check for $10,000. The check did not have a name or an address on it, only a company name. He never revealed to me why he was donating the money, and he never came back again. I didn't believe it was for real, but I had learned not to prejudge anyone. Being skeptical, I did not spend the money until I cashed the check and the money was in our bank account.

Donors came from every walk of life, some gave very little, and some gave a lot, and some gave us things we didn't need at the time, but I always responded gratefully. There were times I didn't have any use for a particular donation, but experience had taught me, if I did not accept their gift, they rarely came back to donate what we did need. A contribution with no strings attached was invaluable. That kind of gift went a long way to help with incidental but essential costs. We sustained the organization on donations and sending a thank you note to every person who donated anything big or small was of utmost importance. I maintain people who are properly thanked for their kindness are often encouraged to give again.

Some in the gay community continued to doubt there were enough children with HIV/AIDS who needed this costly assistance program. They believed I should not be using the very scarce funds which were available to provide services to a population who had comparatively few people in need. I was sympathetic to their position, but it did not negate the fact these children and these families desperately needed help also. Others in the gay community, who Maury and I knew, were very supportive and included Bryan's House in their fund-raising efforts. We gratefully attended every event which was raising funds whether or not Bryan's House was the beneficiary. We went to the Gay Rodeo Association fundraisers, drag shows, fundraisers at gay bars, fundraising parties and fund-raising events large and small.

The doubters continued to come at me from every angle, but I had to stay strong and not let them break my momentum. Sometimes even Lydia doubted my unconventional methods. My

Board stood behind me for the most part, but sometimes they questioned my unorthodox methods, but they went along with them because of the results that I had achieved. I was not prone to follow the traditional ways which most nonprofits adhered to because I was creating a unique organization against all odds. Department of Human Services kept us under their watchful eye. I was under their constant scrutiny because they had stretched the rules to make it possible for us to create a new type of licensing which allowed us to provide multiple types of care in one facility. Funders were skeptical also because we did not have any prior demonstrated experience, but fortunately some were willing to give us a chance because there was an urgent need for these children and families and nobody else was trying to help them.

At the beginning, doctors who were caring for the kids had their doubts about our ability to provide out of hospital care. Before we were in existence, infected children would be hospitalized often, because the key to sustaining these kid's lives was to treat even the smallest signs of illness aggressively. My goal was to provide the highest level of home care to minimize the times a child had to go to the hospital. In addition to hiring a full-time nurse, I applied for a grant which paid for the Visiting Nurse Association to provide extra nursing staff to be able to provide around the clock nurses. Many of the children required ongoing medical treatments so I put systems in place so that they could be administered at the house. Respiratory therapy, daily dialysis, intravenous infusions and accurate and dependable administration of medication were a few of the medically related services we could provide without taking the child to the hospital. We were in constant communication with each child's doctor and earned their confidence in our ability to care for the children. I figured out alternatives to get the medical needs of the children met with limited disruption to their lives. Over time, our care became highly respected by the medical community and time after time we were commended for our expertise in prolonging life.

I had the ultimate responsibility for these medically fragile children. Their lives were in my hands, and there was no room for mistakes. There were times, during medical crises, my nursing staff and I, had to make life-sustaining decisions for these children. Whatever the crisis was, I would get all the information I needed from the professionals to make an informed decision, but ultimately, I had to rely on my instincts. I loved and cared for every child as if they were my own, and at times, the responsibility was genuinely frightening.

The scrutiny I was under was continuous. Sometimes unbearable. Bryan's House was a high-profile project. Sometimes I felt like all the different factions wanted us to fail, especially for me to fail. Constant re-evaluation of the direction I was going in was necessary to make sure I was on the right track. I appeared to be strong on the outside, but a lot of times that's not the way I felt on the inside. Self-doubts and doubts from others can sometimes be helpful and used as a vehicle to effect positive change. Flexibility to change direction had to be maintained to accomplish the goal. I listened to the doubters, but I never let them hold me down. When you are out in front, there are always people shooting at your back, and you just have to duck.

Being a visual person, in the chaos of it all, images would appear in my mind like seeing myself as a juggler, hoping all of the balls would stay in the air and not fall to the ground.

Lydia's health was failing, and her son's health was also deteriorating, as a result, she became further removed from the day to day challenges of our vision.

After Lydia stepped back and was no longer closely involved, the staff began using her as a sounding board for all their complaints. From day one we were existing in a survival mode, which at times was difficult for staff to contend with the unconventional working environment. For many of the employees, it was their first experience working for a nonprofit. They were accustomed to traditional work place, and Bryan's House was the antithesis of a conventional work environment. When staff had gripes, they would try to elicit Lydia's opinions about their complaints which would cause controversy, and petty situations would get blown out of proportion creating discontent.

One such incident which percolated for a while was over some furniture which was donated. The furniture was not anything we could use, and it took up valuable storage space. I gave the furniture to a dedicated child care worker who needed it. There were very few monetary ways I could show my appreciation to a staff person who worked over and above their job responsibilities, so it was my way of showing how much I appreciated them. The furniture was old and battered, and the particular staff person had been working many hours beyond what she was being paid for. I couldn't compensate her financially for her dedication, but I could fill a need which she had. Another staff person, who would have liked to have had the furniture, complained to Lydia about me giving away donations. It became apparent, after repeated incidences of this nature, why Lydia was getting more alienated from the organization.

Staff problems were the bane of my existence. Some of the professionals working for me, who had related degrees in various aspects of the organization, questioned the judgment of my decisions. They had a prevalent undercurrent of superiority which was sometimes obvious. As problems arose and I had to make decisions, I often came up with unconventional solutions. Some of the staff had a hard time dealing with my decisions and would doubt the validity of my judgement. My art school background taught me a creative approach to problem-solving through thinking outside of the box which is invaluable in almost everything I tackle. I struggled with doubts from others at times, but I couldn't let it get in my way. Reminding myself about the ultimate purpose was my antidote to the doubts. I had a passion for the mission, and I was not about to let the doubters sabotage it. I listened to the opinions of the doubters and considered their views in my decision-making process, and ultimately, I would assess whether it was their own agenda influencing the cynics or they had a valid point. At times others input needed to be considered, and with thoughtful contemplation, I would take their opinion into account in my decision-making process before I went forward.

Periodic licensing inspections occurred routinely. They would be unannounced, and each time I would hold my breath hoping everything was in order according to the regulations. Staff and volunteers were busy every moment they were on duty, and it was inevitable some violations occurred. Noncompliance issues often were small issues like somebody leaving a spill in the refrigerator or serving something at mealtime which had not been posted on the mandatory weekly meal menu. It was important to keep as much weight as possible on the infected children and often we had to feed the children something which they would not object to even though it wasn't on the meal schedule. Also, most of our food was donated, and we had to serve what had been given to us on that particular day. It was a difficult problem to adhere to the food regulations. Regulators were accustomed to for-profit enterprises, and there was no room for the fact that we were dependent on donations. Inevitably the inspectors would find issues of non-compliance and would send official reprimands which in a written letter appeared a lot more serious than it was. Rarely was it significant, but there were instances I wish had not occurred. The staff was always working so fast, and furiously sometimes important things fell through the cracks. More significant violations like leaving a medicine cabinet unlocked or a nurse giving a child aspirin for fever without a written doctor's order when she couldn't reach the doctor. Those were the very worst offenses I can remember. Because we were such a controversial and unconventional organization, combined with AIDS being a premier topic at the time, every non-compliance issue would become a story the media highlighted. Passing inspection with flying colors was never newsworthy. The media, although they primarily give us great PR, they were continually hovering around waiting to get a good story about something negative. The small issues, once in print became big issues.

Nearly everything was a learning experience. I didn't allow myself to think about the doubts people had about me. I couldn't, or I would have been paralyzed, and Bryan's House would never have existed.

The second federal grant we applied for turned out to be as troublesome as the first one we had entered into with The People with AIDS Coalition. This time we partnered with Children's Medical Center (CMC) on a demonstration grant. Demonstration grants are usually given to programs which establish or demonstrate the feasibility of a theory or approach to an issue. Generally, these grants are of limited duration. This particular grants purpose was to collect data from pilot projects whose mission was to help women with AIDS keep their families intact. The grant was awarded to only four organizations in the country and we were one of the four. CMC and Bryan's House were the lead project managers for the data collection in Dallas. The funds were to be used for collecting our data and data from other local service organizations who were providing some of their services to women with AIDS. The lead organizations were awarded the major portion of $300,000 each year for three years. The other AIDS service providers received lesser stipends for their data because of their limited participation.

After the first year, it became apparent that participating in the grant was not in our best interest. The amount of staff time devoted to data collection was diverting our primary objective of caring for the children. Most of the money we received was tied to doing studies, not childcare. The staff was overburdened with paperwork from the study which was taking a substantial amount of time away from their responsibilities with the children. I determined the departure from the grant was in the best interest of the children, but politically it had ramifications. The price we paid for declining to participate in the grant was the friction it caused with the other lead manager on the grant who was from CMC. The manager was also one of two doctors on our board and an influential doctor at CMC. Soon after the doctor left the board, and our relationship with CMC became strained. As always, I put the care of the children first and did not let anyone or anything interfere with my commitment to them.

Shortly after I pulled out of the grant, I requested a separate waiting room at CMC for our kids who were infected because they were very susceptible to catching life-threatening illnesses from other patients. It was denied. It was a simple request and in the best interest of the children which led me to believe it was because I withdrew from the grant. Some of the board expressed doubts about my decision in declining the grant and letting go of a source of funding, but I had to stand up for what I felt was right for the kids. Declining the grant resulted in putting us in an adversarial position with some influential people at CMC. My ultimate objective was providing the best care possible to the children and not compromising for somebody else's agenda. Sadly, the price paid for the decision was unintentional enemies.

Again, I had to use my creativity and figure out a way to compensate for the bad blood caused by my withdrawal from the grant. I contacted Parkland Hospital, the county hospital. Parkland Memorial Hospital was literally attached to CMC by a walkway, but it was a separate entity which provided medical care for adults and children. Dr. Ron Anderson, CEO was the administrator of the hospital. He was known as a champion for the poor and the underserved. He was dedicated to the needs of the most vulnerable. From the beginning of the AIDS crisis, Parkland was the first and primary hospital in Dallas which cared for the mounting number of adults with AIDS. Dr. Anderson, a very powerful man in the medical community, was very willing to accommodate the needs of the children. He provided me with a separate waiting room, so the children wouldn't be exposed to other patients. In addition, he provided a medically equipped bus, including personnel, who would come to Bryan's House periodically to provide routine medical care to the children, which prevented unnecessary exposure to others. He was always accessible and compassionate and willing to accommodate whatever needs we had.

Parkland Hospital was also the primary hospital which cared for abandoned infants who were born testing positive for HIV. Before I cultivated a relationship with the hospital, the only alternative they had for these infants was to keep them in the hospital until they became HIV negative or passed away from the disease. It cost the county approximately $800 per day to board these babies at Parkland. At Bryan's House we could care for these infants for $55 per day, and more important, the infants would be in an environment where they would receive the kind of attention all infants deserved.

Leaving the grant caused some dissension amongst the board members but it was my firm belief the negative impact on our ability to care for the children justified the loss of the grant funds. Overtime the relationship with Parkland enhanced our program and consequently the dissension on the board subsided. Many benefits came along with our new relationship with Parkland. We began receiving daily costs of $55 per day to provide residential care to the infants who were moved to Bryan's House from Parkland. The additional funds we received from the county for providing residential care to the abandoned infants subsidized our program on an ongoing basis. Our close relationship with Parkland enabled us to reach a broader population of infected parents who were receiving treatment at the hospital.

Juggling the day to day issues, adhering to all the regulations, and the turmoil of declining the grant was a very stressful time for me. Although making the decision to affiliate more closely with Parkland proved to be advantageous to our program in many ways, it also increased the already strained relationship with CMC. It was a difficult time, but it reaffirmed that I must keep my eye on the mission of providing the best care possible for the children and go forth with determination.

11

THE TSUNAMI OF CHILDREN IN NEED

Barely a breath was taken before I needed to become focused on expanding our space to take care of more children.

As Lydia's disease progressed, she became too ill to continue actively dealing with the overall future of Bryan's House. She and her son Matthew's declining health needed to become her primary focus.

My commitment to Parkland to take care of their infants testing positive to HIV was another incentive to expand our capacity with lightning speed. I couldn't bear the thought that newborns were living in the hospital without being surrounded by loving arms. After completing all the necessary renovations to the existing house, pretty quickly it became apparent that the new cases of HIV were increasing at a rate which would make it inadequate for the number of children who were needing care. I always suspected that would be the case, but we had to start somewhere because initially we didn't have very much money and didn't know what the future needs would be. As soon as we opened, we were bursting at the seams, and each day we were turning away children who desperately needed care.

The next logical step was to raise money to purchase the house we were renting before tackling plans for expansion. Another incentive to move forward quickly was because of the deal we made with the landlord. The lease was signed on July 1, 1988, for the original house and we did not have to pay any rent for July. August, September, and October we only had to pay $600 per month, and after that, we would pay the agreed upon rent of $1,400. We were pinching every penny as it was, and it was in our best interest to find a grant which would enable us to purchase the property as soon as fiscally possible to avoid the $1,400 rent. The original Lease/Purchase Agreement set the price at $170,000 to purchase the property. All along, I hoped we could buy the original house, buy the property next door, and build onto the original home to accommodate more children.

According to health department statistics, when we opened in November of 1988, there were 71 HIV positive children identified in Dallas County, down from 102 in 1987. The discrepancy was either due to the deaths which occurred, or the multiple problems connected to collecting accurate data. Bryan's House mission also included care for uninfected children who were in families with one or more infected family members. It was impossible to predict, with any accuracy, how many people needed our services. Additionally, these families needed various support services at different times throughout their disease process and some ultimately required permanent care for their infected children when they became orphaned. Considering all the variables, it was obvious nine spaces barely impacted the growing number of temporary and permanent care which was needed for these children.

By June 1989, the rapidly increasing cases of infected children became impossible for us to accommodate, even on a rotating basis. Some parents struggling with their own illness were just too ill to take care of their children, and often for them there was no alternative help. It was very complicated for a parent, whether sick or well, to keep a child with AIDS from declining without knowledgeable expert medical assistance. In some circumstances, parents died from the illness, and no relatives were willing or able to take on the responsibility for caring for their children. Adding to the numbers, were the children who were abandoned at birth because the infected mother was unwilling or unable to care for their infant who was HIV positive. Many of these abandoned children were born to drug-addicted mothers incapable or reluctant to deal with their own addiction and a child with AIDS. There was a variety of reasons a child with AIDS ended up as a temporary or permanent resident needing our specialized care. Each child came with their own unique background and needs. Foster care continued to be an unavailable alternative for these children which compounded the need for us to provide a home which included specialized medical care. Each day was a balancing act, we had to continuously make judgments about who we were going to care for that day in our limited space. It was so difficult turning away children who were in such great need of care. We had worked so hard to create a better world for children affected by HIV/AIDS, and after a short while, we were back to where we started, unable to care for the many children who came our way. Expansion became critical and the need immediate. In my preliminary research, when we were in the process of renting the house on Knight Street, I inquired about the adjacent vacant property next door and found out it was for sale. I had high hopes it was going to eventually be our answer for the tsunami of children coming our way. I just never realized how soon the expansion would become imperative.

In September 1989, our census had increased to129 clients. Out of the nine childcare spaces which we were licensed for, five were now being used for permanent residents. Only four spaces were left to accommodate the demand for day care and respite care children. Our walls were bulging, and there was no end in sight for the increasing number of children becoming infected. To increase the number of spaces to 12, we would have to increase the square footage which was being used for childcare. With no other option, the staff had to be moved out of the dining room which was being used as office space. In doing so, licensing permitted us to add three more spaces for daycare if we used the dining room as additional square footage used for childcare. The name of the game was flexibility. Everyone needed to go with the flow and sometimes they were not too happy about it. The Apartment Association of Greater Dallas built a large, badly needed storage building towards the back of the property. It's intended use was for donated items. Donations of goods were our lifeline but storing them was a nightmare. To free up the dining room for child space I moved the staff into the storage building. It was less than ideal working conditions, to say the least. The walls were covered from top to bottom with shelves of donated diapers, baby food, baby bottles, and baby equipment. Staff desks were lined up in a row down the middle. Not ideal but essential.

The house and the yard were finally everything I needed them to be. We had $303,157 in the bank, and 182 clients were competing for services. I temporarily felt financially solvent, but the need to increase our capacity, for the continuously increasing numbers of children needing care, weighed heavily on me. The money we had was not enough to afford the current expenses, the purchase of the existing house, the land next door and the cost to build a building which would accommodate more children. It was a tough sell to convince the board that I could actually accomplish an expansion considering our present financial status, but I had little doubt that somehow, I would make it all happen.

Day to day activities were running smoothly until the night of October 25, 1989. At about 9 p.m., I received a call from the staff person on duty. She frantically announced there was a fire in the house. There were 2 child care workers and five children there at the time. She told me they had evacuated, using the makeshift evacuation ramp, and everyone was okay. The fire department was there, and she and the kids were all out on the street, and she didn't know how much damage had been done. Maury and I dashed into the car and sped down the freeway. When we got to the toll booth at our exit, which was about four blocks from the house, the smell of smoke permeated the air. I then realized this was not just a small fire. I frantically started to try and figure out what I was going to do with all the children and their necessary medical equipment which included a dialysis machine. When we approached, the street was crammed with fire trucks, police cars, and ambulances. The house was dark, and smoke was billowing out of all the orifices. I then saw a sight which still gives me goosebumps when I think about it. The neighbors had run to the rescue of the kids, and each child was in the arms of a stranger. I knew the neighbors were somewhat aware we were caring for children with AIDS because of the publicity from the opening, but until that night I wasn't sure they were sympathetic to our cause.

The house was a mess from the efforts of firefighters putting the fire out. There was smoke and water damage everywhere. It was uninhabitable. There was no time for me to grieve about our loss. I immediately had to come up with a plan for the children. My thoughts quickly went to the question of how that was going to be accomplished. As a quick fix for the night, Maury and I took some of the kids' home with us, and the childcare workers took the others. The next day we had many offers from the neighborhood for spaces which we could use to house the children and staff.

The fire was during the time when many in the gay community were still not too happy about our presence. The tragedy of our fire became another turning point in our relationship with those in the gay community who were opposed to our existence. The next day we were offered a temporary space at the Metropolitan Community Church a few blocks away. It was a community center for the gay community. They allowed us to use a large recreation room which could accommodate all the children and their medical equipment. The bonus was many of the people who utilized the center were eager to help with the children. It helped to ease the resentment which existed in the gay community towards Bryan's House.

After the children were settled, I went to check out the damage and come up with a plan to get back into the house as soon as possible. The fire department determined the fire was the result of a donation we had just received of an environmentally safe air filter for the water heater. As I perused the damage I was devastated, I had worked so hard to make every detail perfect for the kids, and now I had to start all over again. As I was walking around assessing the damage, I heard a faint knock on the door. When I opened it, there was a heartwarming sight which brought tears to my eyes. There stood a group of our Hispanic neighbors with tears in their eyes, adults, and children, each one was carrying an offering of plastic bags full of pennies, nickels, dimes and quarters to help pay for the damage. I gratefully hugged each and every one.

Thanks to all the media exposure, larger donations came in as the word got around. NCNB Bank donated $25,000, Paramount Security systems offered guards to stay at the house until it was secured, and they donated a new fire and security system when the restoration was completed. Everyone's generosity touched my heart, but I will never forget those little bags of money which took some of the sting out of having to redo many of the areas which we had just finished renovating.

12

NO REST FOR THE WEARY

Repairing the damage from the fire and the additional complications involved in caring for the children who were living off-site while I was trying to figure out how I was going to expand our capacity, all made my head swim. The responsibilities kept piling up on me. By that time financial worries had eased somewhat, but after the fire I had to add the expense of the repairs which were not covered by our insurance. Remaining financially prudent was critically important to the plans for expansion. I was always aware of the balance between spending as little as possible on administrative costs and spending enough to adequately run the organization and care for the children. The imperative need for expansion was never far from my thoughts which added to my concerns for fiscal conservatism. To keep the balance, it was necessary for me to take on as much responsibility as possible.

While all that was going on, I remained unwavering in my priority of making sure the children were being cared for with perfection. At the beginning of each day, I would make sure to personally check on each child to make sure nothing related to their care was going on unnoticed. Many times, my days consisted of rushing a child to the hospital, rocking an inconsolable baby, figuring out solutions for a family in crisis, answering the call of Child Protective Services to retrieve an infected child who was in crisis and anything else that came up. Often times, throughout the day, when the stress of the administrative work overwhelmed me, I got my relief from kissing some little toes or sitting on the floor and winding up toys which would make a child giggle. Fortunately, these children had no idea that a heartbreaking scenario loomed over their little lives and when they weren't going through painful medical treatments, they would bounce right back and freely play like any other well child. Despite the fact that death was hovering over the house, day to day life was infused with joy.

Figuring out how to overcome the obstacles which often occurred as a result of creating a unique system of care, was a daily challenge. I was always walking a fine line trying stay in compliance with all the traditional regulations while managing a unique system of care. Programming was in continual flux as the needs of the families changed. Almost daily the children and families would present an unanticipated situation which needed a unique solution. Existing services regularly required adjustment to make sure we were meeting the needs of all the clients.

We remained the only organization whose mission was to meet the needs of infected women and children therefore, I constantly had to lobby society to recognize and support this populations needs. Courting the affluent for their support, managing the media, appeasing the medical community, and contending with all the unexpected daily occurrences was an important ongoing process.

Dealing with the media felt like an all-consuming job in itself. Initially, it was not my area of expertise, but I had to quickly become proficient at it. There was a constant flow of reporters covering every event at the house no matter how small. It was necessary and valuable to get as much exposure as possible to raise money and to let the infected community know our services were available to them. AIDS was a significant topic of the times, and the media was obsessed with writing about anything related to the issue. Through trial and error, I gained insight into the art of giving an interview spontaneously. It was a difficult challenge not to say something which could be misconstrued or taken out of context. Reporters would often show up at the door, and no matter what I was doing, I would have to stop and give them undivided attention.

While the number of families and children in need were rapidly swelling, I had to quickly figure out how we were going to expand. We had the original house, which we didn't own, and I needed to figure out how I could purchase it. I had my eye on the piece of land adjoining it which seemed to be the most logical answer to our need for more space. At this point, there were no guarantees the owners would be willing to sell it to us or whether we could raise the money needed to buy it and build a building on it. We were turning away children daily, and still, it was impossible to get valid numbers of children requiring care. Again, I was in a constant state of anxiety trying to figure out how I was going to be able to accomplish this next huge step.

My ongoing image of being a juggler continued to haunt me. I saw myself balancing many swirling plates on the top of long sticks, imagining if one fell, everything might come crashing down.

By January 1989, our walls were bulging, and it was clearly apparent that there was not one more inch of space to expand the existing house. It was time to act and come up with a plan to somehow extend the capacity of our services. In the back of my mind, I had always imagined the property next door was potentially our next step. Considering we did not own the existing house, thinking about purchasing the additional property was a bit of a crazy idea, but I had faith I could pull it off, and it was absolutely necessary to accommodate the onslaught of children needing care. Fortunately, most of the board had faith in me because of what I had already accomplished, but as always, there were those skeptics who had their doubts. Again, the search for additional funding began, but this time I needed a lot of money to execute the future plan.

The property next door was a corner lot adjacent to the original house. It had two shabby houses on it which looked like a strong wind could blow them over. The houses were being used by vagrants for drug trafficking. The lot was owned by First Latin American Assembly of God who initially had a church on it which burned down. The Reverend of the church, David Lara, was building a replacement church on a different site and lucky for us, needed additional funding for the completion of it, so he was motivated to sell it. Also, the city was fining the church every month because of the two abandoned houses on it, which gave us more leverage. We were in a good bargaining position, and the Rev. Lara was supportive of our mission. I struck a deal with him that we would demolish the houses and clear the land so the church would not continue to accrue fines. In exchange, he agreed to allow us to use the property until I could buy it.

My grand plan to clear the lot ended up being easier said than done. I was sure the volunteers could remove the houses piece by piece. They looked shabby, but they were sturdy. We tried to use chains attached to vehicles to pull them over, but they wouldn't budge. We huffed, and we puffed, and we made no headway. I finally had to concede and pay professionals $750.00 to remove the structures. Continuing to reassure Rev. Lara that I was going to be able to buy the property as soon as I raised the money for it, he allowed me to put a 10-foot wood fence around the entire property encompassing the land around the original house. The extensive wood fence gave the appearance of one large property providing security and anonymity to our clients. Of course, I got the fence donated including an automatic gate with an entry keypad for additional security.

All the details of how to purchase the first house, the land for the new building and the construction of an additional building, again caused sleepless nights. The new property had to be rezoned for our specific use, which meant the surrounding neighbors had to be persuaded not to object to our plans. I found out the process typically leads to some objections and controversy and each person who opposes needed to be personally convinced to approve the rezoning. I also had to appear before City Council to make a case for the need to rezone. Additionally, the new land and the land the original house was on needed to be re-plated to be one property. Another process which was foreign to me!

I applied to the Meadows Foundation for funding for the construction of the new building. The foundation was prone to fund bricks and mortar, but not land. The grant was accepted contingent on the purchase of the land and it came with the caveat on the funding which required us to begin the building process in three months or we would lose the funding. It then became my urgent priority to find funding for the land, so we did not lose the Meadow funding for the building. The purchase of the existing house had to be put on the back burner for the moment for my plan to work out.

As the project evolved, it was a challenge to quell the board's uncertainty about my decision to go ahead in the planning of the addition considering we did not yet own the original building. We also had not secured the funding for the land the new building was to be built on. Some on the board doubted my judgment on the plan, but I pushed on, and as each piece of the puzzle fell into place, they began to stand behind me. As usual, flying by the seat of my pants, I persuaded the board to go forth with the planning. My strategy was once I found funding for the land, we could begin to build the new building securing the Meadows funding and then I would go after the remaining piece of the project which was to purchase the original house. To reassure the board and as a precaution in the event I couldn't find the funding for the original home, I devised a removable enclosed walkway which would link the two buildings and could be removed if necessary. The detachable walkway reassured the board, and they were comfortable going ahead with the construction of the new building knowing we could separate the two properties if we needed to. We needed as much space as we could get because the number of children was continuing to increase, but if I had to make do with just the new building it still would have been a drastic improvement. Fortunately, the owner of the existing house did not have a problem with connecting the new building to the house which he still owned.

Tom Higier, the Chair of the Board after Maury, was a real estate attorney who was a fortuitous help in the negotiations of the land. Another board member, Nancy Nasher, a synagogue member, came to the board with considerable experience in real estate matters. Amongst many of her other philanthropic endeavors, she and her well-known family built and owned NorthPark, a major mall in Dallas. This team of experienced board members in the matters of land accusation were an invaluable asset in obtaining the land.

The 28,743 sq. ft. new land was listed for sale for $250,000. After Tom's negotiations, the land cost us $170,000. As part of the deal we had to put $55,000 down, and the church financed the remainder at monthly payments of $1,020. A reasonable payment which our budget could accommodate until I got a funding source, or sources, to pay off the balance.

I immediately went to work on finding sources to pay off the land. Contributions from NCNB Bank, the Dallas Cares fundraiser, Hoblitzelle Foundation, Hillcrest Foundation, Society for Abandoned Children, DIFFA, Highland Park United Methodist and a block Grant from the City of Dallas paid off the remainder of what we owed for the land. We then received the Meadows funding for the building, and we were able to begin the construction of the new building.

The ground-breaking ceremony was on a sunny afternoon in March of 1990. The newly acquired land, surrounded by the very tall new wood fence, was crowded with people. The anxious media was interspersed throughout the crowd anticipating the announcement of the next step in the evolution of Bryan's House. The surrounding Red Bud trees were just beginning to show their tiny little blooms signaling a new season was to start. Similarly, we were about to embark on a new season in the evolution of Bryan's House. The children were all dressed up and giddy. They were excited by all the activities even though most were too young to understand what was happening.

The excitement grew as we waited for the arrival of our Master of Ceremonies, Mayor Annette Strauss, who was one of our faithful supporters. After I did a short welcome speech, Tom Higier, introduced Mayor Strauss. Lindsay Cushingberry stood by us representing a child with AIDS who would benefit from the services which Open Arms, Inc. provided. Mayor Strauss began by saying "AIDS comes in all colors. AIDS comes in all sizes. AIDS crosses all age, race and socioeconomic barriers." She went on to say "In 12 months the number of children served has increased by 260%. As of December 1989, Open Arms, Inc. had served 216 clients, although not all were for childcare. Thanks to the medical advances and also to the quality of care given at Bryan's House, these children are living longer. The client population was not dying as fast as we had expected. Faced with this disturbing growth in client population and with the limited capacity of Bryan's House, Open Arms began planning - with the same "can do" attitude - the urgently needed expansion of the facility." She finished up by saying "Dallas can be proud of this model project. Bryan's House is unique across the country. It is a replicable model, and Dallas has the advantage over other cities which do not offer this comprehensive service. Inquires come to

Open Arms from many parts of the nation, even from around the world. The word has spread about a place called Bryan's House. With our yellow hard hats on and shovels in hand, Mayor Strauss, Tom Higier, Lindsay and I dug the first dirt which would soon be the future of Bryan's House. Maury stood close by holding Beth dressed in her little pink hooded jacket.

At the end of the ceremony, our faithful supporters from DIFFA provided a reception. In DIFFA's typical fashion, the reception was an elegant affair. Steve Burrus, Executive Director of DIFFA, who gave me the seed money which gave birth to Bryan's House, was at the helm orchestrating the event. As the lively event went on, I tried to thank each and every supporter who took part in furthering the mission of Bryan's House.

As the crowd dwindled, I had a moment of realization about the fantasy which had run through my mind when we first rented the original Bryan's House. My thoughts of expansion, to the vacant land next door, were about to become a reality. I thought about the little glimmer of hope I had, of someday being able to acquire the adjacent piece of land for the certain growing numbers of children who needed care. Vivid visions came to me as I stood there imagining that my plan was about to rise up out of the earth. We were off and running to the next chapter in the life of Bryan's House, and we were going to be able to care for more children who were in dire circumstances.

*M**aury** and Mayor Annette Strauss holding Beth at the ground-breaking ceremony for the new building.*

Designing the new building to function efficiently was an exciting prospect. With my creative background, it was an aspect of the process I thoroughly enjoyed. The efficiency of function and visual appearance were my priorities, and I had the opportunity this time to create it from the ground up. Working with Chris Rador, the architect, my goal for the new building was to be able to accommodate all the needs of the staff and especially the children. Finally, the staff was going to have a legitimate workspace. The plan was to use the existing house and convert it into offices for the team. From the start, we had to take what we had and make it function the best way we could. I now had the luxury of designing a facility which was built to meet the specific needs of our population and the staff. After many meetings with the staff, we hashed out specifics which would help them perform their jobs in the best way possible. The original staff had to make do with our impoverished and less than desirable working conditions which they endured because of their dedication to the children. It was very gratifying to finally be able to give them a comfortable and efficient working environment.

Plans were evolving for an additional 5600 sq. ft. building, attached by a walkway, to the existing house. The new building was to be two stories to expand the available space as much as possible. At the rear of the building, there would be a covered, fenced in, 5200 sq. ft. outdoor play area. To the back of the play area would be a secluded parking lot. The exterior of the new building was replicated to look like the Tudor style of the original Bryan's House for continuity. Both structures were painted light blue with darker blue trim to give the appearance of one building. The first floor would be used to accommodate 40 children for care and the second floor would be adult space for support groups, counseling, storage, activities and possible housing for older children.

To complicate matters, again I had to obtain new licensing because of the increased number of children we would be caring for. But this time, I knew how to play the game. We would no longer be designated as a Foster Group Home. The new license designated us to be a Special Care Facility requiring us to follow an entirely new set of rules.

Upon completion of the new building, the staff would move out of the storage building and actually have fully functioning offices in the original house. We were becoming more like a traditional organization which helped improve the morale of some of the staff who had trouble dealing with the way we had to initially function.

The beginning of the foundation which would connect the new building to the existing one.

As the building process went on, the children were thriving. The numbers of children desperately needing care were still dramatically increasing. There was continued heartbreak every time we had to turn away some very needy children, but now there was light at the end of the tunnel.

On October 13, 1990, we finally were able to move into the new expansion. It was one month short of two years from the opening of the original building.

The dedication ceremony was on November 30,1990.

The interior of the new building carried on the theme of bright primary colors. A horizontal array of windows lined the walls. This time the windows were constructed to meet the correct specifications, so they did not have to have plexiglass on them. Light streamed in from every angle.

The entryway to the new addition was in the rear of the building with access to the parking lot. It provided a confidential and safe entrance for the clients to pick up and drop off children without being visible from the street side.

The entrance from the rear parking went directly into the new building. Turning left from the entrance led to the walkway of the old house which became offices, segregating administrative activities from childcare. Upon entry, to the right, was a reception area for parents and volunteers to check in. One of the many luxuries we did not have in the existing house. The separation reduced the chaos which previously existed with adults and children all trying to function in the same space. The result was an overall sense of calm. There was a meeting room off the reception area which was used for support groups, staff meetings, and board meetings.

Next was a fully equipped nurses office, which included two additional rooms designated to separate sick children from other childcare areas. These rooms were invaluable in an environment catering to children with compromised immune systems. Of primary importance, these rooms enhanced our ability to prevent illness from spreading to the larger group of children.

Separate girls' and boys' bathrooms with showers were decorated with red, yellow and blue tiles completely covering the walls for sanitation purposes. Every surface was designed to be easily sanitized to control the spread of illnesses. Opposite from the bathrooms was a long hall with observation windows which flanked the large activity room where most of the children's activities took place.

The Lindsay Activity Room, named for Lindsay Cushingberry, Dorothy's infected granddaughter, was furnished with everything the ideal, well-equipped day-care center could hope for. On the opposite side of the play room was a bank of windows which looked onto the outdoor play yard. The surface of the playground had a recycled rubber surface which was typically used for tennis courts. I was able to convince the manufacturer to donate it in exchange for publicizing the unique use of their product. The rubber surface limited the potential risk of bleeding from typical childhood bumps and bruises. An important factor when bodily fluids were a danger to caretakers, volunteers, and uninfected children.

Adjacent to the activity room was another bathroom designed for the youngest children. Child size toilets, small bathing tubs and diaper changing tables were essential for caretakers in the never-ending task of keeping children clean and dry.

There were separate bedrooms for girls and boys for temporary and permanent overnight care, each had five toddler beds in the room. The bedrooms were furnished with the same red, yellow and blue themed decor which was prevalent throughout the building. If it weren't for the number of beds in each room, they would have looked like any privileged child's bedroom. Bright murals, painted by a local artist named Siros, covered the walls with red hearts and yellow chubby figures dancing around the walls of the room.

The nursery for the youngest children had 10 cribs and 4 rocking chairs. At the far end of the room was an enclosed padded play yard with rubberized climbing forms customized for the littlest ones. Custom window coverings matched the brightly colored fabric wall hangings which adorned the walls.

The kitchen was equipped with efficient commercial appliances allowing Dorothy to be able to create her delectable home-cooked meals with ease. She was now preparing meals for 40 children a day as opposed to meals for 12 children. The adjoining dining room had high chairs and customized tables adapted for feeding multiple toddlers at one time.

The laundry room was well equipped with several washers and dryers to keep up with the never-ending loads of laundry.

There was a designated room for the night duty staff which had direct access into the boy's and girl's bedroom areas which enabled caretakers to keep a watchful eye on sleeping children. The room also included a private area for confidential files, so caretakers would have details of each child close by.

All of the furnishings and equipment were donated by various funders. In our fundraising efforts we challenged donors to fund the interior of an entire room and in return we rewarded them with a plaque of appreciation outside the door of the room they funded.

By September 1991, I had raised funds for the purchase of the original house at 2713 Knight Street.
According to the original lease purchase/agreement, we received credit for the rent payments we had already paid, and the remaining cost was $160,000.

On January 8, 1991 all the parts of the expansion puzzle culminated in a unique facility encompassing thoughtful relevance and innovation. Defying all the doubters, Bryan's House had finally evolved from a grassroots effort, in a tenuous battle for survival, to a model program answering the needs of a neglected population of women and children with HIV/AIDS. Purely out of compassion and relentless determination the struggle to survive was achieved. The new facility accommodated many more children in need and was the epitome of efficiency. Many of the difficulties which had to be contended with in trying to function in a residential house with minimal capacity, adapted for a child care facility, were alleviated.

Finally, having raised $655,788, I felt secure about finances, and it was a new era in the life of Bryan's House.

13

THRIVING BEYOND EXPECTATIONS

Planning and construction were an intense responsibility for me on an already full plate, but I couldn't let it distract me from my top priority of maintaining the health of the children. There was a fine line between life and death for these children and any change in their medical condition could have grave consequences.

Cassie thrived at Bryan's House. She became an entirely different child from the time I picked her up from the Galveston hospital. Little by little she made strides, and it became apparent her deficits were not nearly as severe as we were initially told by the hospital staff. We were continuously working on things which would give her quality of life. My daughter Kim knew sign language and was able to teach Cassie some signs to communicate instead of her spitting or having a tantrum to express her needs and emotions. As time went on, she eventually became somewhat able to communicate in sign language. The little girl who was so incapacitated when we picked her up at the hospital became a happy little girl with a greatly improved quality of life. She came a long way because of the tender loving care she received from everyone at Bryan's House. With therapy, she learned to walk with a walker and eventually on her own. She responded to touch, and she began to love to be hugged. By 5 years old, the little girl they said would not live longer than a month, was able to board a school bus for the handicapped and go to special education classes.

In the beginning, I was wary of Bobby, Cassie's dedicated surrogate parent. His reputation as a troublemaker subsided, and everyone came to realize he was motivated purely out of love and caring for this little human being. Bobby finally trusted I had Cassie's best interest at heart. For years he flew up to Dallas almost every weekend to be with Cassie. In her stroller, he would take her out on excursions to parks and malls. The outings were the highlight of her life. Those two had their own method of communicating. Without Cassie having the ability to speak and with limited hearing they were able to communicate with each other on a level beyond anyone's understanding. Finally, after seeing Cassie's progress at Bryan's House, Bobby told me "as hard as I fought in the beginning to keep Cassie in Galveston, I will now do whatever I need to do to keep her at Bryan's House."

Bobby died of a heart attack when Cassie was six years old. From his death on, Cassie had an aura of sadness she could not articulate, but it was apparent to anyone close to her. She never truly understood why Bobby left her life. One year later, almost to the day, Cassie died.

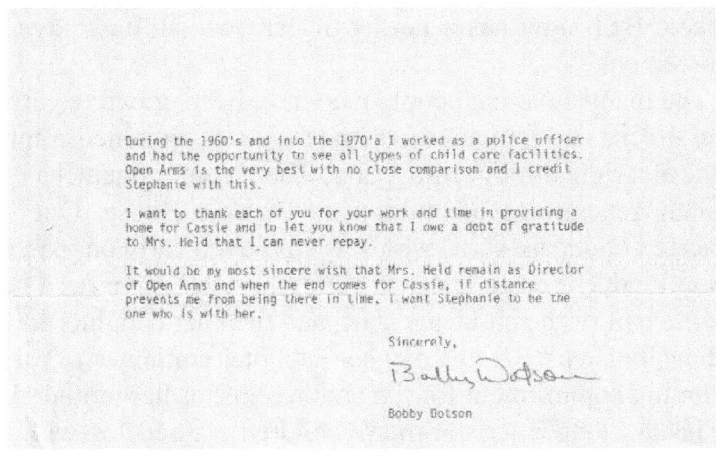

A heartfelt note from Bobby to Stefanie.

Beth, who spent most of her first year in my arms, converted to HIV negative and became eligible for adoption. In spite of the fact that she was absolutely healthy, CPS still did not have anyone willing to adopt her because of the stigma surrounding the disease. Maggie, one of the first child care employees at the house, loved and cared for Beth also and decided she wanted to adopt her. As Maggie was going through the process of becoming eligible to adopt her, CPS decided they would move Beth to another facility in case the adoption was not approved. Their justification was it would be easier for them to find another permanent home for her if she did not have the stigma of living at Bryan's House. I adamantly contested their decision to move her from the only family she knew while they were waiting for Maggie's adoption to be finalized. It became a significant conflict with CPS. Maury tried every legal channel to stop her removal from Bryan's House, but we had no grounds to stand on. She was in the custody of the state, and they had every right to remove her. It was clearly not in her best interest, and to prevent them from removing her, I had to allude to the fact that my only option was to expose the injustice to the media. CPS finally conceded, and she was able to stay until Maggie got approved to adopt her. Maggie then adopted a little boy who she fell in love with at Bryan's House. She is a loving and extremely committed person who gave these two children the family they so deserved. Maggie now volunteers at Bryan's House faithfully as "grandma," sharing her love with the many children in need. Beth now has a family of her own and is studying law enforcement.

The many amazing people who have been drawn to caring for these special children have in some instances remained committed to the mission through the years. Their commitment has lasted through generations of children at Bryan's House. One of the dedicated childcare staff, who was employed early on, passed her loving kindness on to her own children. After she retired her son became part of the childcare staff, and then her daughter followed in their footsteps. To this day her daughter continues to carry out the loving commitment for the children just as her mother did.

Today, long after the many children I cared for with AIDS have passed away, only one child, who is now an adult, is still alive and fighting the disease. It was over thirty years ago when I met Lindsay and her grandmother Dorothy who were in dire straits at the time. They were ostracized, in need of money and Lindsay was critically ill. Lindsay's life has been a courageous battle for survival. Continuous medications, hospital stays, and torturous treatments run her life, but somehow, she manages to smile in between bouts of illness. Much of Lindsay's longevity is attributed to the lifelong loving and attentive care from her grandmother Dorothy. Dorothy educated herself on every treatment which came along to fight the horrific disease. When the National Institute of Health discovered a treatment that seemed like it had the potential to treat the disease, Dorothy didn't hesitate to take Lindsay to Washington, DC to participate in it. Every sneeze, every cough, every fever would get Dorothy's full attention, and off to the doctor they would go. Dorothy fully realized it would take an immediate response to any change in Lindsay's health to keep her healthy. I believe it was Dorothy's will and tenacity which has kept Lindsay with us today. Her dedication and love for a granddaughter, she never planned on bringing up, has been beyond admirable.

In 1992, Lydia succumbed to the disease. Her brave fight for herself and the many lives she touched live on in the hearts of many. At the time of her death, AIDS was still very much a secret from society, and Lydia requested that the cause of her death not be mentioned at her funeral. Even after her life, she remained vigilant in keeping her secret, so she could protect her son from being the target of the prejudice which was still prevalent. Matthew lost his fight for life in 1995, just a month before his 13th birthday.

After the completion of the new building, my own life abruptly shattered.

14

AN UNBEARABLE LOSS

On April 26, 1991, which happened to be my birthday, and twelve months after the first shovel of dirt was dug for the expansion of the new facility, I took Angela to CMC for medical care. She was not looking well, and I wanted her to be checked out. A few days before, Maury had mentioned he didn't feel quite right, so I suggested he make an appointment with his doctor. When I questioned him about what he meant when he said he wasn't feeling quite right, he told me he was having trouble doing his daily ritual of completing the NY Times crossword puzzle. His statement didn't make much sense to me because it seemed so vague. He made an appointment with his doctor who examined him thoroughly and concluded there was nothing wrong. To ease Maury's concerns, the doctor suggested he should get an MRI on the Sunday following his appointment with the doctor.

On Monday morning before we left the house, I asked Maury, who was the picture of health, never missing his daily workouts and never even having as much as a cold, how he was feeling. He said he was okay. Shortly after, we got a call from his doctor who said he needed to change Maury's follow up appointment which was scheduled for the end of the week. The doctor explained he had to go out of town for the rest of the week. The doctor asked him to come in that afternoon.

When I got to CMC with Angela, I called Maury to let him know where I was. Cell phones had not become the mode of communication yet, and I wanted him to know where I was if he needed me. It wasn't because of any health concerns on my part. We always kept in contact with each other throughout the day. When I reached him, I asked how he was feeling because I sensed he wasn't feeling quite right that morning even though said he was okay. His response to me was "I'm not doing very well today." I suggested he call the doctor. His answer was "I can't remember how to use my phone."

At that moment my world came to a halt, and it was obvious something was seriously wrong. I called the doctor, and he told me to get Maury and come in immediately. All of sudden I felt like a fog had taken over my brain. My state of mind darted from fog to panic. In my total confusion, I managed to call Bryan's House and get a staff person to come be with Angela. While I waited for the staff person to arrive, I called Maury's boss and asked him to take Maury to his doctor, and I would meet them there. I could barely think straight. I didn't know what to think. All I could focus on was I had to get my car from the valet and get to Baylor Hospital which was about 2 miles away. As I drove faster than I had ever driven, I was struck with the thought that my life was about to be shattered.

At the doctor's office, we found out Maury had a brain tumor called Glioblastoma. The doctor told us that the nature of the particular type of tumor increased in size rapidly. He informed us the MRI revealed the tumor had invaded about half of his brain. The doctor said it was inoperable because of its size and the tentacles were intertwined in most of his brain. Still, in shock, random thoughts were dashing through my head. How can this be! He seemed fine! The doctor then rendered the death sentence. Maury only had about three months to live.

The doctor immediately admitted Maury to the hospital which was right next door to his office and said he would do a biopsy the following day. We walked in silence. Both of us confused and in shock.

I called my trusted friend, Rabbi Liza, and asked her to get Kim and Josh and bring them to the hospital. Kim was working at the Dallas Theater Center, and Liza went and told her what was going on and brought her to the hospital. Josh was a freshman at the University of Texas in Austin, and Liza arranged for Kim to fly down to tell him the devastating news and to bring him home.

The diagnosis was the most crushing moment of my life. The love of my life, the person who I saw across the room and instantly knew we were destined to join our souls as one was being torn from my life. As Kim and Josh entered the hospital room, and I looked into the pools of tears in their eyes, it tore my heart apart even more. They unequivocally adored this man whose wisdom sustained us all. Everyone who ever encountered Maury had a sense there was something extraordinary about him. It was a devastating loss for everyone whose life he had touched.

The next hours are still a blur. Friends started arriving in the hospital room in droves. They brought food and set up a bar in the room. No one ever left. The next day Maury was taken to surgery for a biopsy. When he came back from the biopsy, he was still somewhat woozy, and he asked me what the results were. As we stood there holding on to each other I told him, "It's the worst you could possibly imagine" his immediate response was "well lets party till the end." His bravery was extraordinary. Never a complaint, or a why me.

As the brain tumor continued to grow, Maury's faculties remained pretty much intact. The doctors told us that once the tumor invaded his brain stem, it would end his life. Two weeks before his death he began to have a headache, which was a sign that the end was near. We moved into the hospice section of the hospital and Maury lapsed into a coma. Again, crowds of friends and relatives began accumulating to stand vigil day and night. His room and the long hall outside his room overflowed with people. Some never left for the entire two weeks he lived in a coma. The hallway outside his room was littered with sleeping bags, hospital pillows, and blankets which were used for respite by friends and relatives.

Everyone knew the end was imminent after fourteen months of living on borrowed time. Maury's spirit manifested itself in each and every one there. Complying with Maury's wishes of partying until the end, there were few tears in our presence from the people around us during those two weeks. Everyone did what they could to keep our spirits up. Our friend Sara Hickman, a well-known Texas singer, sang and read to Maury as he laid in his hospital bed in a coma. Maury's doctor spent time in his room playing guitar. Friends brought in a television and played his favorite movies. The well-known Dallas restauranteur, Javier, sent elaborate meals accompanied by coordinated cocktails. Maury was loved and admired by everyone he ever encountered, and it was apparent until the end. Maury lived fourteen months from the time he was diagnosed after we received the life-shattering death sentence. Fortunately, he was not debilitated during those way too short fourteen months of life we had together after the diagnosis. He had an amazing spirit. Rarely were there any more tears, we just put one foot in front of the other and partied till the end.

There is a part of me which considers myself lucky because I got 27 years of life with this extraordinary man.

On June 1, 1992, Maury died at 45 years old.

Maurice Louis Held

When Maury was first diagnosed with the brain tumor, all my attention turned towards taking care of him and my children. My life took an abrupt turn, and my priorities shifted to my family. Bryan's House was firmly established. I had succeeded in raising $2,000,000 from my first attempt to raise the money to support my vision of caring for the young children of the AIDS crisis. When I left there was a full year of operating expenses in the bank, and I felt confident Bryan's House could go on successfully without me.

As the bleeding from my broken heart subsided it left me with a scar which will never go away. It then became time to figure out how I was going to go on in my new life. The only way I knew to go on was to immerse myself in something meaningful. Luckily, in August, a new adventure presented itself. More accurately, I leapt into a new challenge which piqued my interest. My salvation was to engage in something distracting.

Two months after Maury died, I took on a new adventure. For me, taking on a new challenge was the antidote for my grief. The distraction of trying to accomplish something new helped me to build a new way of being without Maury by my side. The portion of my heart where Maury lived and still does live has a crack in it which can never be fixed. Dwelling on the grief would not erase any of the pain, and I was determined not to let it stop me from living a purposeful life. Finding a new opportunity and getting involved was my salvation. Again, putting one step in front of the other and moving forward to build a new life helped me gain the confidence that at some point, I was going to be able to survive without Maury. I did have lapses into the darkness of my aching heart sometimes, but somehow, I managed to pick myself up and keep moving forward. Thinking about my next adventure helped me to look to the future and not sink into the sadness. From time to time, I did have doubts I even wanted to go on without Maury. When those dark thoughts tried to creep into my head, I thought about what Maury had said to me before we had an inkling a large mass was taking over his brain. On a particularly sunny day, several weeks before the horrific diagnosis, while we were chatting during one of our routine drives to work, Maury said: "If anything happens to me, you have to promise me you will go on." Needless to say, I sat there in total shock wondering what provoked such a morbid statement. I was a bit irritated that on this picture-perfect day, when everything seemed fine, that he would say those shocking words. In retrospect, on some subliminal level, he must have sensed something was wrong. I did promise him I would go on and it wasn't until a long time after he died that I remembered that bewildering conversation.

Throughout Maury's illness, friends Mary Jane Redington and Tom Fry moved in with us to do whatever needed to be done to help us get through this mind-numbing time. They remained by our sides throughout the fourteen months until death took Maury from us. Shortly after, they both had the opportunity to go to Little Rock, Arkansas to work in Bill Clinton's Campaign Headquarters. Mary Jane's mother, Mel French, a longtime friend of the Clintons, was the manager of the campaign headquarters. A week or two after Tom and Mary Jane went to Little Rock, I went to visit them, and the fascinating chaos of the campaign swept me away. Even though politics had never interested me, getting involved in a campaign for president was just the distraction from my grief that I needed. Initially, I volunteered to work on the campaign. I didn't have any idea what I was going to do there, but it was an exciting atmosphere, and it was just perfect timing to get involved with something all-consuming. The frenetic pace of the campaign headquarters was apparent as soon as I walked in the doors. Everyone there had a critical job to do in the election process. It felt like the heartbeat of our nation was beating right there.

The campaign offices were jammed full of busy people, many whom I recognized from their presence on television. Of course, Bill, Hillary, and Chelsea Clinton were constantly present with notable people like George Stephanopoulos, James Carville and Wolf Blitzer who were all doing their jobs with intensity. There was a constant underlying imperativeness which dominated each, and everyone's assigned task, but to the outside observer, there appeared to be an orderly casualness of typical life on a campaign. It was not an unusual site to see James and George in thoughtful contemplation, barefoot and bouncing a basketball, as they pondered critical campaign issues.

AIDS was still a very controversial issue and a hot topic in politics. As it turned out, my background and knowledge in this hot topic became known, and I was appointed to be the point person to handle AIDS-related issues at the headquarters.

At that time, AIDS and gay were synonymous in some people's minds, so in addition to AIDS issues, my position included overseeing any gay volunteers. Dictated by ignorance, a lot of people assumed if someone was gay, it was likely they were infected; therefore, my presence was highly valued because a lot of people were shying away from anyone who was gay. We worked seven days a week from early morning until we were about to collapse. Being at the heart of our country's politics was exciting. I had previously not given much thought about the dynamics of politics and how the political machine worked. It was an enlightening experience intriguing me to this day. The experience gave me the opportunity to work with some people who were national legends in the world of AIDS. One of which was Cleve Jones. A legendary AIDS and LGBTQ rights activist and the creator of the Names Project. The Names Project was a compilation of small squares of fabric sewn together, memorializing people who had died from AIDS. Initially, the quilt traveled from city to city in memory of those who were no longer with us. Now, the quilt weighs 54 tons, and because of its size, it no longer travels around America and is permanently on display in Atlanta, Georgia.

During my work at the campaign, I also had the opportunity to utilize my artistic background and was asked to design an AIDS lapel button. The button was distributed at a campaign rally during Bill Clinton's famous speech in New Jersey which targeted the AIDS crisis. As with most things during the campaign, the buttons had to be accomplished at lightning speed. I designed and supervised the production of the lapel button in 24 hours, making it ready for distribution the next day during the candidate's speech. The buttons were flown to Bill Clinton in New Jersey on a private jet only carrying the buttons and the secret service escorting them.

Everything during the campaign was done fast and furiously, and fortuitously it left me little time to dwell on my broken heart. The morning of election day began an exciting culmination of everyone's intense work. The day started with everyone having to leave the campaign headquarters, so the secret service could sweep the building for anything which might be dangerous to a potentially new president. It began a very long day of tension and anticipation. Nothing more could be done to win the race. It was a whirlwind of excitement as the day progressed, and election night was the epitome of it. As we stood outside in front of the big stage watching the results from each state come in, and be tallied up, the rain was torrential. Hardly anyone noticed we were drenched from the rain when the win was finally confirmed.

The next day there was a momentary lull after all the excitement of the big win until it became apparent a whole new experience was lurking just days away. We mistakenly thought the freneticism had come to an end, but almost immediately it became time to close down the campaign headquarters and head to Washington to plan the inaugural activities. Just a little over six months after Maury died, I found myself on a plane heading to Washington, DC as a part of Bill Clinton's transition team. Mary Jane and I arrived in DC and were assigned offices in the Washington Naval Yard and lodging in the Mayflower Hotel with other campaign officials. Upon arriving, my assignment was to design and implement the interior of a full-blown retail store for the inaugural memorabilia. The store had to be open and fully functional in two weeks. After the hectic completion of the official inaugural store, I again thought my life was about to slow down, but almost immediately I was hired to design two catalogs for the merchandise which was for sale in the store. One of which would be included in the invitation to the inauguration. The task was quite daunting considering I designed it on my bed without a proper drawing board or any of the implements which I typically would have used to produce a catalog. It was a nail-biting experience to create a nationally prominent piece of artwork, which was going to be sent to everyone invited to the inauguration. Typical of campaigns, it all had to be accomplished at a dizzying speed, which by then I had become used to the hectic pace. The bonus at the end of this ecstatic experience of being on the campaign trail was the opportunity for my children, my friends, and me to go to the inauguration ceremonies and all the spectacular inaugural balls.

Of the many memorable experiences which I had during my campaign adventure, one stands out as a cherished highlight. During the day that the actual inauguration ceremonies were to take place I was in the White House as the Republicans were moving out and the Democrats were moving in. Everyone was very busy readying the building for the new administration and I had the privilege of being able to wander around and see this iconic building unimpeded by restrictions. Amongst the many daunting sights was President John F. Kennedy's initials which he had carved inside the top drawer of his desk.

Life has a way of inspiring you and giving you direction if you step outside of your comfort zone and participate in the world around you. I was determined not to let the grief take over my life. Making the conscious decision to take on something new helped me focus on living in a new way. A way without Maury.

When I returned from Washington, I pondered what new experience I was going to embark on next. I had created a new life for myself, and I was moving on. Bryan's House was doing just fine without me. It had a board of directors and a new Executive Director and a life of its own apart from me. AIDS was still raging in the gay community, and the number of straight people who were becoming infected was increasing. My continued commitment to help through the AIDS crisis remained important to me, and I was elected to the board of AIDS Services of Dallas, ultimately becoming the Chair of the Board. In light of the increasing number of cases of AIDS in the community at large, the idea occurred to me, that making condoms available in bars, might help to increase the awareness of the threat of contracting the disease and hopefully save a few lives. Many in the straight young adult community, weren't knowledgeable about how AIDS was contracted and were still under the assumption AIDS was strictly a gay disease. To raise awareness and hopefully enlighten this coming of age generation, I purchased used condom dispensing machines. I refurbished them, designed subtle warning messages to be prominently displayed on them and installed them in the bathrooms of bars.

Shortly after, another opportunity emerged because of my experience working on the Clinton campaign. A friend and Bryan's House board member, Paula Larsen, who was a family law attorney, embarked on running to become a judge and asked if I would be her campaign manager. Although I had just been involved in the political arena, I did not have any experience in running a campaign, but as usual, I studied everything I could about it and went full steam ahead.

Life is so full of choices if you can force yourself to put your doubts aside and have the courage to get involved. Excitement awaits around every corner if you just put yourself out there and explore. One of my favorite things to do, when I reach a crossroad in my life and have no immediate goal, I go to the bookstore and meander around reading excerpts from random books. Curiosity often spawns motivation. At times it would seem like a subject would jump off the shelf and I would get entrenched in an idea, and I would know what I was going to do next. That is how I got into buying rental properties. I picked up a book on the subject, and it enticed me. I bought all the books I could find on the subject and taught myself everything I needed to know about the process. I started my own company and named it Holland Investment Properties, Inc. Holland was the street I lived on. I ended up buying and managing 47 rental units. Financially it was great, but it didn't satisfy my creative or my altruistic aspirations. After a while, it was time to move on to something which did fulfill me.

During this time, the all-consuming endeavor of being a property owner, rental agent, and manager, my kids were married, and my grandchildren were born. My son Josh was married to Sasha, and they had a baby boy named Jakob and a second son named Maxwell. My daughter Kim married Christopher and became pregnant with triplet boys.

Moving on in my personal life became complicated. Life cycle events intervened, and my family needed my full attention again. My parents were aging, and their health was deteriorating. As their health problems exacerbated, my parents began requiring more assistance from me. My mother was starting to show signs of Alzheimer's and my dad's heart was weakening. I put a pause on my own life and focused on taking care of their daily needs. As my mother's mind became less clear and she became more dependent, my dad's heart became increasingly damaged. During my dad's next to last hospitalization before he died my daughter delivered premature triplets.

My daughter gave birth to the triplets three months before her due date. Their survival was tenuous from the start. I was trying to keep everything in balance, but once again heartache enveloped my world. My days became split between tending to my parents and doing all I could to help my daughter and son-in-law while the babies were battling for their lives.

The triplets were born at 26 weeks. At birth, Nathaniel weighed 1 lb. 4 oz., Matthew was 2 lbs. and Andrew was 1 lb. 8 oz. All barely hung on to life for months. They all had life-threatening medical abnormalities. Time after time each baby would stop breathing and would have to be brought back to life. My life became devoted to helping care for these tiny, fragile babies while I was managing the care of my parents.

Initially, all the babies were in incubators and on ventilators to breathe. Drew was born with his intestines on the outside and had surgery his first day of life. They each had holes in their hearts requiring repair. They couldn't eat naturally and had to be fed through a tube in their stomachs. Their eyesight was compromised. For months, while they remained in the hospital, we would watch the numbers on the monitors which indicated how each one was doing. Intermittently, the horrifying sounds of alarms would blare, alerting that one of the babies was not breathing and life-saving measures had to commence immediately. As they improved, they came home one by one. Nate, the tiniest, had the most severe medical problems and was the last one to come home. Finally, all three were home just in time for them to celebrate their first birthday. For the first time, they were all together in their nursery at home. The walls of the nursery were bright yellow with hand painted animals which Christopher, a muralist, diligently painted on the walls while we waited for the boys to be well enough to come home. It looked like a typical nursery until the babies arrived, then the cheerful nursery was anything but ordinary. The room was crammed with medical equipment, ventilators and around the clock nurses. As time went on Matt and Drew's medical complications improved but Nate continued his fight for life and eventually needed a lung transplant. In Matt's fifth year of life, he was diagnosed with Autism. Periodically, each one would have a medical crisis, related to their prematurity, and emergency medical intervention would become necessary. Nate's life continued to be very tentative. He was in and out of the hospital and struggled every day of his life to live. The constant 911 calls to save his life became part of our routine. The emergency medical teams would come rushing into the nursery, and the other two boys would stand up in their cribs to watch the activity as if it was a normal occurrence. Kim and Nate would be rushed off to the hospital and Matt, and Drew would lie back down and drift off to sleep. 911 emergencies would occur regularly necessitating bringing Nate back from the brink of death. Other times we would go a few months without a life-threatening emergency. It became our way of life to resume some sort of normalcy in between the traumas.

While Kim and Nate were away at various hospitals in Dallas and Houston, my son-in-law and I would care for the other two boys. My mother reached the point that necessitated her being moved to a nursing home, and my routine became supervising her care while often carrying a baby boy on each of my hips. My mother fell deeper and deeper into the darkness of Alzheimer's and eventually died from a traumatic fall from her wheelchair.

At eight years old, Nate lost his battle for life.

Nathaniel Louis Arnold

As Matt and Drew got stronger and needed me less intensely, it was time for me to distract myself from the sorrow by taking on another endeavor that excited me. It was time to undertake a challenge I could focus on. As usual, my antidote for getting through the sad and sometimes agonizing times in life was to embark on something consuming. It was not in my nature to wallow in the depths of despair and allow the emotional pain of the circumstances to keep me down. During the difficult eight years leading up to my mother, father and Nate dying, when time allowed, I distracted myself from the heart wrenching daily routine and finally focused on my original aspiration of becoming a painter. After Nate's death, I opened up an art gallery with my friend Mary Jane. We named it MJ & S Fine Art Gallery. It not only gave me a vehicle to display all the paintings I had done over the eight years while I was devoting my time to my family, but it allowed me to pay homage to my dad's life's work by displaying his paintings alongside mine.

Some may believe my experience at Bryan's House was a plan from a higher power to prepare me for what was ahead with the triplets. Whether you ascribe to that theory or not, my time at Bryan's House provided me with the skill and knowledge needed to be a valuable component in the day to day life-sustaining efforts for my own medically fragile grandchildren. It seems ironic that at the same time my personal life became focused on my own special medical need's grandchildren, Bryan's House mission began including similar children who had a variety of special needs. As the number of children affected by AIDS was decreasing, because of the advancements in prevention and treatment, Bryan's House expanded its mission to include children with special needs who are not able to attend traditional childcare. The existing program which was created to provide childcare to HIV/AIDS children and support services to their families is a unique model which perfectly suited the unmet needs of families whose children have special needs.

15

THE GIFT OF GIVING

We are our choices. A simple act of kindness, or an endeavor to rectify a world problem, defines our character. Giving of oneself reaps an immense emotional satisfaction and the intangible rewards are bountiful. For me, compassion for people with AIDS grabbed my soul and compelled me to act when I became aware of the horrific impact it was having on the lives of a population who was unsuspectingly subjected to an atrocious nightmare. A situation which touched my soul so profoundly that I felt I had no choice whether or not to risk my own safety to make life tolerable for a population who was being tortured by unimaginable despair. With a fierce determination to help those afflicted, I took action to make a difference and the self-gratification continues to fill my heart with joy.

At first, I set out to help those who I personally had encountered. I never envisioned, that in the future, my actions would impact so many. To date, Bryan's House has directly and indirectly impacted thousands of children and their families. I will never know just how many lives it has influenced as a result of variations of this model program being replicated around the world.

Every act of altruism, regardless of whether it is celebrated or seemingly inconsequential, has the potential to break the cycle of discourse which is encompassing society today. Helping one person in peril or participating in a cause which impacts the lives of many, is a means to a more peaceful world.

The Merriam-Webster Dictionary defines altruism as "showing a selfless concern for the well-being of others." Showing concern for those in need and acting to alleviate their pain, has immeasurable impact. The immense self-gratification received, from selfless acts of kindness, can help one rise up from the darkness in their own life. Helping someone out boosts self-esteem. A selfless act of kindness can increase the joy in one's own life, potentially contributing to emotional well-being.

Research indicates that when we are showing compassion, the hormone oxytocin is stimulated, resulting in a calming effect. Increased oxytocin is thought to reduce stress, make one happier and increase longevity.

Acts of altruism may not come naturally to some, but it can be cultivated by anyone in pursuit of a more meaningful existence. Its effects can result in giving life its most profound significance. According to Psychology Today "Acting with unselfish regard for others doesn't always come naturally, even though many psychologists believe we're hard-wired for empathy. After all, cooperative behavior did allow our ancestors to survive under harsh conditions. But most of us realize that when we make an effort to give without expectations of reciprocity, we feel fulfilled and energized."

Taking action to make a difference in the world can empower one to have confidence in their own abilities. Acts of compassion towards others, is a powerful antidote to the despair felt when you are going through your own hard times. Realizing your power to improve the lives of others can transform not only their lives but can lift you up from your deepest darkest place. During times of depression, when feelings of being lost and alone are overwhelming you, taking on something which matters, can lift you up beyond expectations. It can lead to surprising adventures and unconsciously drive out despair. At times of hopeless confusion, reaching out and finding something meaningful to get involved in can lift up spirits beyond imagination. We often do not have control of the devastating events which occur in our own lives, the only power we have is how we are going to deal with those times. Focusing on traumas or difficulties, which are beyond one's control, keep one immobile. Helping others in need can transform that darkness and lift you up through troubled times. Promoting positive change in the world can facilitate a person's own healing. Discovering your value to the world around you instills a powerful sense of self-worth. Having a positive impact on another's life can transform your own life. Even a small act of kindness can have a significant effect on changing someone else's destiny. The payback for your actions, in helping others, leads to a deep sense of self-worth. Achieving self-worth goes a long way in lifting you up through your own difficult times.

Life is often just busy. Henry David Thoreau notes, "It's not enough to be busy. So are the ants. The question is: What are we busy about?" If we are fortunate enough to not be encumbered by devastation beyond our control, one can have the ability to structure their life to have meaning and not just existence. How have you spent your life? Take a look back, it doesn't matter what stage of life you are presently in. There's always time to create a legacy that will live on beyond you. Ponder whether you have had a meaningful life, or have you just been in the pile of ants doing busy work. It's unlikely you will be satisfied for just being busy unless your life has been meaningful.

Are we too busy to offer a helping hand? By taking the time to act on a simple act of kindness, a person may alter another's life beyond expectations. In turn, the intangible reward is an extraordinary sense of accomplishment.

I recently observed a woman at the airport who seemed to be having a difficult time. I was rushing to get into the line to get my tickets when I noticed her in the line in front of me. She stood out to me because she was crying and looked disheveled. She was covered with a multitude of tattoos, which were very apparent because of her skimpy clothing. There was an inappropriate distance between her short shirt and her torn jeans which was exposing her frayed underwear. Her hair was splashed with red, blue and green colors. Her only luggage was her duffle bag which was quite dirty, and it appeared to have already lived a long life. Although her appearance was enough to catch my eye, her agitation and the tears of black eye make-up streaming down her cheeks made it apparent that she was having a difficult time. The airline attendant was trying to calm her down, and I overheard the tearful women say she was trying to get to a rehabilitation facility. From what I overheard, it seemed to me, that she was conflicted about her decision to try and restart her life. The attendant walked away, and I got distracted with trying to move forward to get my ticket. When I turned back around the woman was gone. When I got to the departure area, I checked the waiting room where her plane was due to depart. I realized she hadn't made it to the flight which might have altered her life. Maybe with a little encouragement and support from a stranger, she could have had the strength to get on the plane to a new life.

Occurrences like this can easily be ignored in our busy lives but taking a moment to reach out can have a significant, meaningful impact on the life of another. Most often we'll never know whether our actions had any positive effect, but the willingness to try is what matters.

The opportunities to help out another human being are frequently present. They may appear to be an effortless act of kindness or as a great solution to a problem which can have an everlasting impact on the world. Both ends of the spectrum and every action in between will not only provide help to those in need but will give you a deep inner sense of accomplishment that your life on earth has had a positive impact.

A woman appeared at the door of Bryan's House one day. It was clear to me from my experience that she had all the visible markings of a person with full-blown AIDS. Her cheeks were sunken in, and her skin was marred with sores, presumably from the AIDS-related cancer, Karposii Sarcoma. Behind her was a grocery cart parked on the sidewalk with all her worldly possessions cascading out. Her body was frail, exposing her prominent bones which were apparent signs of a combination of illness and homelessness. Her appearance was disturbing. Her hair was knotted and dirty. The dress she was wearing was so worn the paisley print was barely visible, and she only had one sock on. When I answered the door, she said she needed diapers for her baby who was at Parkland Hospital. Of course, what she said didn't make much sense because if the baby was at the hospital, the baby would have diapers. I gave her the diapers she was asking for, much to my staff's objections. They objected to what I did because they felt she was just going to sell the diapers. It was obvious this woman was down and out, and she needed some help. It was not for me to judge the actions of this woman, only to recognize she needed help. A few boxes of diapers were a small price to help out this woman who apparently was struggling to survive.

Something as effortless as handing a dollar, or whatever one can afford, to a panhandler on the street corner, can make a difference in a stranger's life. Maybe that dollar will help put food on the table for the beggar's children or perhaps it will buy desperately needed medication or maybe it will buy them a beer. We have no idea when we encounter a person for a few seconds as to why he is begging on the street. The only thing we can be sure of is the person is living a difficult life, and we have the opportunity to make it a bit better. We can be judgmental and think this person is lazy or worthless or just wants the money for drugs or alcohol, but maybe not. For all the dollars I have given out, if a few people were using the money for inappropriate reasons, then so be it. The vast majority have fallen on hard times, and for those people, I have effortlessly helped make a difference.

Tragic situations exist all around us and they can be so easily ignored when they don't personally affect us. If we turn a blind eye and do not show compassion to others, how can we expect for others to come to our rescue when we are in need? There are times we notice someone else's suffering and we feel bad for a split moment, and then we go back to being involved with our own busy lives. There's not one day we don't hear about tragedies like the ravages of war around the world or a person on a street corner that someone noticed needed help. Every day in this country and around the world, adults, and children are starving. Young women are being abducted for sexual exploitation. Minorities are being judged and persecuted daily. There is no lack of tragedy in our world! We often feel powerless because there is so much need it becomes overwhelming and therefore, we do nothing. If we are lucky enough to have been born into circumstances which do not require us to fight for our own survival, then we have the power to make a difference in someone else's life who is less fortunate. Showing up to help when we perceive there is a need has the power to open amazing doors in our own life.

With enough perseverance, we can have an everlasting impact on this world in some way. Even if one is broken down and tired, there is always someone who is more broken down and tired, and we can make a difference in another's life. Get involved, reach out and it will undoubtedly help you to rise up from your own problems. Courage to help someone else can give us the gift of purpose in our own life. Choosing to live a life of kindness, in an intentional meaningful way, will result in finding contentment in your own life.

Discovering your purpose in life will undoubtedly infuse you with a deep sense of exhilaration. Pay attention to the world around you and notice the occurrences which cause a spark within your soul. Make a move in the direction of that spark, and it may lead you to places you never imagined. Whether you are choosing to take a path which will make a difference in someone else's life or you are tackling an injustice which will better the world, it will have a powerful positive impact on your own life. It might be the life you are living is not the life which satisfies you. It has no purpose. It's never too late to redesign how one wants their life to be. The actor Henry Winkler insightfully said, "To be rudderless is painful." Embrace uncertainty and find your passion. Each step towards your goal will enhance your confidence. With each success, you will gain power, and it will propel you to achieve great things.

When you perceive an injustice in the world, don't just complain about it, do something to change it. Everyone has the power to create change. It takes hard work, courage, and determination but accomplishment will instill a deep sense of gratification in your life. One of Mahatma Gandhi's insightful statements challenges us with his words. He proclaims, "you must be the change you wish to see in the world." It may be that the thought which sparks your interest, is your intention to tackle a world injustice or maybe it is a plan to improve the life of an individual. It might even be a burning desire to invent a new widget which creates a business which would provide you with enough money to contribute to helping others change the world. The process to success in accomplishing your goal takes intention and perseverance but finding your purpose in life can give you far more than what you have given.

Discover your purpose by taking notice of that fleeting image which ignites passion in your spirit. Seize the moment. Be proactive, go for the person you want to be and don't look back at the episodes which have previously blocked you from accomplishing your dreams.

Don't wait to take some sort of action towards the thought which ignited your interest. Begin by participating in situations where you can explore the path which will take you to your destination. Learn all you can about it. Envision how you want it to look in the end result. Before committing to your endeavor, assess whether the end result is indeed something which excites your soul and motivates you. You have nothing to lose. You can always change your mind and go on to the next endeavor which sparks your excitement. When you've made up your mind, go full steam ahead! As time passes, enthusiasm fades and doubts invade your psyche. Set timelines for achieving each step towards your goal. Without firm timelines, an idea just remains a fantasy and eventually withers on the vine. Your life is a blank canvas in front of you. Picture how you want the canvas to look in the end result. Whatever endeavor you choose, envision what you wish it to look like when you accomplish it. Act and begin drawing out the steps which will complete the picture.

Surround yourself with people who have related experience and interest in your endeavor. Volunteering or offering your help without pay most often opens up doors. Connect with like-minded people and go to activities which are related to your interest. Show up for what you believe in. Recognize the helpers, there are some in every crowd. Those are the people who will lead you in the right direction and be there to support your dream. Every conversation is education. The people you encounter who stand out in the crowd, and who show interest in what you are doing, could be the people willing to help you towards your goal. President Bill Clinton once said, "figure out what needs to be done and get people to come along with you." Push past the gatekeepers and the doubters, which for one reason or another, want to sabotage your enthusiasm. Keep your eye on your goal and push forward.

Don't focus on the doubts that it can't be done. Figure out ways to get around the obstacles. Think outside the box to come up with the solutions. Focus on your goal and experience the excitement in figuring out how to get there. Let the details about how you will accomplish it take over your thoughts. Imagine it in your mind's eye, see the end result of your goal and make a plan to get there. Let it take over your mind and become absorbed in it. As your goal is formulating in your mind, be meticulous in the details of your plan. Research every aspect of it. Get the knowledge. Search the internet. Browse through a bookstore or library on related topics which can give you insight into the bigger picture surrounding your idea. Read random bits and pieces which might give you a broader view of your goal.

Gather the helpers and pay attention to their input. Use their feedback as information but don't let their doubts stop you. Use their doubts to identify the obstacles and figure out how to get around them. When you've obtained the knowledge, plan a logical step by step approach to accomplish the end result of your endeavor, then *take action*. As you travel through your journey to make your impact on the world, your plan as you see it, will sometimes need to be altered. Adapt your path to accommodate the circumstances which you had not anticipated, but don't give up. Focus on the end result and keep your mind open to changing the details to get to it. Never let the obstacles deflate your dream. Be passionate and let the world see your excitement. It's contagious!

Every reasonable person has self-doubt. Sometimes that doubt is essential to reevaluate what one is doing to make sure you are on the intended path. You may have to alter your path but don't let doubt stop you. Defy the doubters but pay attention to their input and judge for yourself if there is any validity in what they are saying. Defy the doubters, don't let someone else's doubt about you, be your doubt about you. Don't own their doubt, it's not yours, it's theirs, and they can keep it, you don't have to.

Rarely does one hear entrepreneur and philanthropist in the same context. It is perceived that entrepreneurs set out to make money and philanthropists just want to do good. It is a misnomer to think they are mutually exclusive. Whether volunteering or monetarily reaping the financial rewards from your intended goal, the creative process of accomplishing it is the same. It takes hard work, thoughtfulness, and tenacity. Both the philanthropist and the entrepreneur are the ones who solve the problems. They have courage and insight and are willing to risk failing. They are the big picture people who learn from their failures and rise again until they succeed. Figuring out solutions to yesterday's mistakes will teach you how to solve tomorrows problems. There isn't anyone who doesn't make mistakes. Mistakes are part of life's lessons which contribute to future success. Move ahead with passion and conviction and you will succeed.

"You make a living by what you get, but you make a life by what you give. Thus, in going about their voluntary activities, individuals are also cultivating an outlook that contributes to a social environment that nurtures the well-being of all." - Winston Churchill

Bryan's House is my masterpiece. Each brush stroke it took, was worth every moment of hard work and emotional torment I went through to complete the final picture. Not any part of it felt like it was a sacrifice on my part, only a feeling of immense privilege to have been a part of easing the pain of so many. For me, the all-encompassing sadness I felt when I became aware of the deadly virus which was bestowed upon men, women, and children with AIDS was relieved by taking action to help. From picking up tiny newborns from the hospital who nobody wanted, or giving peace of mind to a dying mother, gave me the gift of knowing I lived a worthwhile life. Forging forward, to do what needed to be done during that untenable time, helped me to dry my tears. It ignited a powerful determination within me to defy all the doubters who thought this herculean idea could not be accomplished.

Now, when I enter the doors of Bryan's House, 30 years from the time I welcomed in the first child in peril, I think about every child who I loved and lost. In my mind's eye, I don't see the anguish on their faces, I only see their smiles and hear their laughs. Some, because of their disabilities, had silent laughs, but just about all could smile. Their smile reaffirmed they felt cared for and loved. These little ones were fortunate because they were too young to understand the terrible disease which had incapacitated them. Unfortunately, the adults with the disease were not so lucky.

They lived with the excruciating physical pain of the illness and the emotional pain of watching their loved ones suffer and deteriorate from the disease. For them, I feel confident that I did everything possible to help them on their journey to the end of their life.

As I walk down the halls now, my heart swells with pride when I see a new generation of medically fragile children benefiting from the seed I planted. Children who would otherwise be neglected by society because of their special needs. Children whose parents can now provide for their families because there is a place their special needs children can receive the medically managed care Bryan's House provides. The playrooms are still continuously filled with children laughing and playing in a safe environment with other children who have similar needs. Children who are not alienated because of their differences. I still can't help gravitating to the ones in most need. As I sit on the floor cradling and consoling a child in need of comfort, I feel the presence of a warm glow enveloping me. The very same feeling I felt holding every child I helped through the years.

I never imagined, when I opened the doors of Bryan's House, that all these years later, this children's haven, would still be helping care for fragile children and their families suffering from life-altering situations.

30 years ago, I reached down and picked up a pebble, and with all my might, threw it into a pond. And to date, the ripples of that pebble have now helped more than 23,000 children and their families.

EPILOGUE

The enduring mission of Bryan's House continues to provide care for the population of affected children and their families impacted by HIV/AIDS. Today 31% of children in care are from families affected by the disease.

From the beginning, parent support services proved to be a lifeline for families dealing with a disease which complicated every element of their existence. Although the number of infants and young children with HIV/AIDS has dramatically declined in the United States, parents with the disease are still gravely affected.

Presently, the Center for Disease Control and Prevention (CDC) estimates 1.1 million people in the United States are living with HIV, including 1 in 7 (14%) people who are unaware of their status. Approximately 40% of new HIV infections are transmitted by people who are unaware that they have the virus. The Foundation for AIDS Research (amfAR) states, "The proportion of AIDS diagnosis amongst women has more than tripled since the early years of the epidemic."

The research for a routine vaccination and a cure continues. Until these answers are found, the virus will not be eradicated. HIV/AIDS is now considered to be a chronic disease as opposed to a terminal disease because of the effective strides in the treatment of the disease. People living with the disease can now take a minimum of medication, replacing the multitude of life-sustaining medications which were required at the onset of the epidemic. Fewer medications have resulted in more infected people adhering to their medication routine, which is imperative for prolonging life.

The drug Pre-Exposure Prophylaxis (PrEP) has been developed to reduce the chances of an uninfected person contracting the disease from an infected person. If taken daily by the uninfected who have high-risk behavior, it can dramatically reduce the chances of contracting the virus. Unfortunately, the use of this drug is not widely known and not used consistently by most people at high risk.

Today, the number of cases of infected heterosexual people, in lower socioeconomic populations, has increased disproportionately from the onset of the disease. A contributing factor is the lack of affordable medical care which prevents this population from obtaining routine medical care and therefore, the infected unknowingly are spreading the disease. Additionally, the out of control drug epidemic which is now occurring in our country, is also a significant factor contributing to the spread of the disease amongst the addicted population.

Adolescents are also a population at high risk due to the lack of information being disseminated to this new generation of the sexually active. AIDS is no longer a prominent topic, and many adolescents are unaware that the disease is still a threat which could impact their lives. Additionally, this younger population often feels infallible and therefore dismisses the consequences of participating in risky behavior which could lead to contracting HIV/AIDS.

In the beginning, when infected children reached preschool age, they were banned from entering schools because of the perceived risk to other children and school staff. It took activism and education to create change for these voiceless children to be allowed to go to school. As Bryan's House staff actively disseminated knowledge about the routine use of universal precautions which prevents the spread of contagious illnesses in schools, the ban began to change. Our lobbying for change resulted in it becoming mandated that these infected children be accepted into mainstream education.

As the disease evolved and treatment improved, the infected children were no longer facing death at an early age, and it became necessary to adapt Bryan's House services to a longer-term approach to care. Maintaining our commitment to adapting to the current needs, in 2000, we implemented a preschool education program to prepare the infected children to go to school.

As the infected children were growing up, programming was initiated to meet the needs of infected adolescents. In 2001, a program was developed to help infected teens deal with an array of important issues which affect a teen living with the disease. The program also included education and support to newly infected teens. The teen program provided camaraderie and social interaction with other teens dealing with the complex issues of living with AIDS.

As the HIV/AIDS population changed and the need for assistance to very young children with the disease diminished, Bryan's House staff realized the existing medical model could incorporate another unmet need in the community. In addition to continuing to serve the HIV/AIDS population, the program now includes young children with a variety of specialized medical needs who are unable to attend traditional childcare due to their condition. The unique model program, which had been created to serve the AIDS population, has become a lifeline for families trying to cope with these under school-age special needs children. Many of the existing support services provided to infected families are similar to the kind of support services needed by parents with special needs children. Without the services of Bryan's House, parents often are unable to work, attend school or generally provide for their family. The ability to have their children in an environment which expertly provides medical intervention and therapies which meet their children's individual needs, often enables parents to go from being impoverished to living a successful life.

Having a medically complex child strains a family emotionally and financially, often resulting in the separation of parents or in some situations, abuse or neglect of the children. The unique programming enables parents to improve their lives while their medically challenged children are in an appropriate setting which meets their childcare needs. The parents in need are assisted and counseled by professional staff who help them to find a way forward while contending with their challenges. Parents with children who were born or developed medical complications which would prevent them from attending traditional childcare outside of the home, now have a medically managed system to rely on.

Bryan's House has maintained the philosophy of caring for children and their families when there are no services in the community who specifically meet their needs. The program employs experts in medical, educational and therapeutic intervention increasing the potential of each child in care. Families who live stressful and complicated lives due to their children's limitations are provided daily child care. Respite care is also provided for these families when life gets just too hard to cope with. Without regard to the nature of the children's disabilities, needy children are always welcomed with open arms to Bryan's House.

While routinely meeting the needs of this underserved population, Bryan's House also provides emergency care for children with special needs when an unexpected crisis occurs. These special needs children often fall through the gaps of desperately needed specialize care during emergency situations. Recently, that safety net was there to provide care for an unexpected population of families with special needs children who were in desperate need of help during a very disorienting crisis. Hurricane Harvey bludgeoned Houston, Texas, in September of 2017. During the hurricane, Mother Nature intervened in the lives of Houstonians, destroying lives and causing catastrophic havoc. In unprecedented numbers, volunteers across the country banded together to do whatever they could to help in the effort to save lives. Ordinary people risked their own lives to save strangers. Others gave money and donated items to help ease the emotional and physical devastation which the victims were struggling with during the crisis. Many stepped outside their own safe lives and became saviors. One of those saviors is the current Chief Executive Officer of Bryan's House, Abigail Erickson Torres, who recognized the lack of services for special needs children of displaced families who were living in shelters in Dallas. She immediately made plans to accommodate these special needs children at Bryan's House. Families with medically fragile children faced additional challenges living in shelters with their children. Once again, Bryan's House was there with open arms, offering a safety net for the most vulnerable of children. During the hurricane, in the spirit of Bryan's House, Abigail's innate compassion compelled her to reach out to these children. It was her empathy and dedication to the original mission of Bryan's

House which compelled her to action. Abigail's foresight and Bryan's House's ongoing intent became a lifeline for these traumatized families. With immediate action, the tired and scared special needs children were rescued from the chaos of the shelters and had their unique needs met in a loving environment. Bryan's House remains dedicated in its commitment to offer a helping hand and be the wind beneath someone else's broken wings.

I have immense gratitude for every person who has, and still, participates in maintaining Bryan's House as a haven for children and their families during the perilous times in their lives. The mission could not have been accomplished without all the people at the beginning who had open minds, open hearts and open arms. People who put their own fears aside to come to the rescue of a desperate population. I am thankful for every person who has sustained this mission by contributing financially and who freely give of their time to improve the quality of life to all who walk through the doors. The enduring success of this unique endeavor is largely attributed to the many community supporters. Nancy Roe, Linda Hall, Dr. Lisa Genecov, Rust E. Reid, Jean Raub, Temple Emanu-El, Paul Riddle, First Lady Laura Bush, and many, many other long-time board members have faithfully sustained the backbone of the organization. The staff, all of who are deeply committed to the life sustaining care of the children are commended for their dedication and their intense hard work. I am deeply grateful for the continuous cadre of volunteers who have never wavered in their commitment to the mission of providing comfort and a way forward for families who have nowhere else to turn for help. Each and every person who has been dedicated to the organization, and faithfully kept the mission alive has my heartfelt appreciation.

My commitment to Bryan's House remains steadfast, and in my heart, I will always cherish the memories of every child who I loved and lost to this cruel and unrelenting disease. Despite all the heartache and hard work, it took to accomplish this mission, it undoubtedly remains one of the most gratifying experiences in my life.

Bryan's House can be contacted at (214) 559-3946 or by going to bryanshouse.org.

Made in the USA
Monee, IL
30 August 2020